First World War
and Army of Occupation
War Diary
France, Belgium and Germany

21 DIVISION
Headquarters, Branches and Services
Royal Army Ordnance Corps
Deputy Assistant Director Ordnance Services
23 October 1915 - 31 May 1919

WO95/2140/2

The Naval & Military Press Ltd
www.nmarchive.com
Published in association with The National Archives

Published by

The Naval & Military Press Ltd

Unit 10 Ridgewood Industrial Park,

Uckfield, East Sussex,

TN22 5QE England

Tel: +44 (0) 1825 749494

www.naval-military-press.com

www.nmarchive.com

This diary has been reprinted in facsimile from the original. Any imperfections are inevitably reproduced and the quality may fall short of modern type and cartographic standards.

© **Crown Copyright**
Images reproduced by permission of The National Archives, London, England, 2015.

Contents

Document type	Place/Title	Date From	Date To
Heading	WO95/2140/2		
Heading	21st Division Dep. Asst Dir. Ordnance Services Oct 1915-May 1919		
Heading	D.A.D.O.S. 21st Div Vols: 1,2,3		
Heading	War Diary of D.A.D.O.S. 21st Division. From 23/10/15 To 31/10/15		
War Diary	Merris	23/10/1915	31/10/1915
Heading	War Diary of D.A.D.O.S. 21st Division. From 1st Nov. 1915 To 30th Nov. 1915		
War Diary	Merris	01/11/1915	08/11/1915
War Diary	Pont-De-Nieppe	09/11/1915	30/11/1915
Heading	War Diary of D.A.D.O.S. 21st Division. From 1/12/15 To 19/12/15		
War Diary	Pont-De-Nieppe	01/12/1915	19/12/1915
Heading	D.A.D.O.S. 21st Div. Part Of Vol. 3 Dec 1915		
Heading	War Diary of D.A.D.O.S. 21st Division. From Dec: 18 1915 To Dec: 31st 1915		
War Diary	Armentieres	18/12/1915	31/12/1915
Heading	D.A.D.O.S. 21st Div. Vol. 4		
Miscellaneous	Oi/C A.O.D Section		
Miscellaneous	D.A.A.G.I.	25/02/1916	25/02/1916
War Diary	Armentieres	01/01/1916	07/01/1916
War Diary	Pont-De-Nieppe	08/01/1916	31/01/1916
Heading	D.A.D.O.S. 21st Div. Vol. 5		
War Diary	Armentieres	01/02/1916	08/02/1916
War Diary	Pont-De-Nieppe	09/02/1916	29/02/1916
Heading	D.A.D.O.S. 21st Div Vol 6		
War Diary	Pont-De-Nieppe	01/03/1916	21/03/1916
War Diary	Merris	22/03/1916	31/03/1916
Miscellaneous	D.A.G. 3rd Echelon	11/06/1916	11/06/1916
War Diary	Ribemont	01/04/1916	04/07/1916
War Diary	Belloy Sur Somme	05/07/1916	08/07/1916
War Diary	Cavillon	09/07/1916	12/07/1916
War Diary	Mericourt	13/07/1916	20/07/1916
War Diary	Le Cauroy	21/07/1916	30/07/1916
War Diary	Duisans	30/07/1916	31/07/1916
Miscellaneous	April 1916 Missing		
War Diary	Duisans	01/09/1916	04/09/1916
War Diary	Le Cauroy	05/09/1916	13/09/1916
War Diary	Ribemont	14/09/1916	14/09/1916
War Diary	Carcaillot Farm	15/09/1916	03/10/1916
War Diary	Ailly Le Haut Clocher	04/10/1916	07/10/1916
War Diary	Hoeux Les Mines	08/10/1916	12/10/1916
War Diary	Labourse	13/10/1916	28/12/1916
War Diary	Labeuvriere	29/12/1916	31/01/1917
War Diary	Wormhoudt	01/02/1917	01/02/1917
War Diary	Bethune	09/02/1917	15/02/1917
War Diary	Labourse	16/02/1917	15/03/1917
War Diary	Lucheux	16/03/1917	28/03/1917
War Diary	La Cauchie	29/03/1917	19/04/1917

War Diary	Bois Leux Au Mont	19/04/1917	29/04/1917
Miscellaneous	D.A.G. G.H.Q. 3rd Echelon	11/07/1917	11/07/1917
War Diary	Boisleux Au Mont	01/05/1917	20/08/1917
War Diary	Duisans	26/08/1917	12/09/1917
War Diary	Caestre	15/09/1917	23/09/1917
War Diary	Meteren	23/09/1917	30/09/1917
War Diary	Micmac Camp Near Quderdom	01/10/1917	05/10/1917
War Diary	Blaringhem	08/10/1917	19/10/1917
War Diary	Chateau Segard Ypres	23/10/1917	14/11/1917
War Diary	Vieux Berquin	16/11/1917	16/11/1917
War Diary	Barlin	18/11/1917	22/11/1917
War Diary	St. Catherine Arras	24/11/1917	30/11/1917
War Diary	Tincourt	01/12/1917	06/12/1917
War Diary	Roisel	08/12/1917	08/03/1918
War Diary	Longavesnes	18/03/1918	18/03/1918
War Diary	St. Denis	22/03/1918	22/03/1918
War Diary	Maricourt	23/03/1918	24/03/1918
War Diary	La Neuville	24/03/1918	25/03/1918
War Diary	Allonville	29/03/1918	01/04/1918
War Diary	Dranoutre	03/04/1918	07/04/1918
War Diary	Dickebusch	10/04/1918	14/04/1918
War Diary	Hooggare	15/04/1918	16/04/1918
War Diary	G14.b. 8.2 (Poperinghe)	17/04/1918	30/04/1918
War Diary	Bouvancourt	27/05/1918	27/05/1918
War Diary	Faverolles	28/05/1918	28/05/1918
War Diary	Romigny	28/05/1918	29/05/1918
War Diary	K 6,5.4 22	30/05/1918	31/05/1918
War Diary	Chaltrait	01/06/1918	03/06/1918
War Diary	Congy	04/06/1918	09/06/1918
War Diary	Les Bordes	10/06/1918	14/06/1918
War Diary	Ecoivres	15/06/1918	15/06/1918
War Diary	Martinneville	16/06/1918	22/06/1918
War Diary	Gamaches	23/06/1918	01/07/1918
War Diary	Beauquesne	01/07/1918	25/07/1918
War Diary	Raincheval	26/07/1918	25/08/1918
War Diary	Mailly Maillet	26/08/1918	04/09/1918
War Diary	Beaulencourt	05/09/1918	20/09/1918
War Diary	Rocquigny	21/09/1918	30/09/1918
Heading	War Diary D.A.D.O.S. 21st Division October 1st-31st 1918 Vol 37		
War Diary	Fins	01/10/1918	11/10/1918
War Diary	Walincourt	12/10/1918	22/10/1918
War Diary	Inchy	23/10/1918	08/11/1918
War Diary	Berlaimont	09/11/1918	30/11/1918
Heading	War Diary of D.A.D.O.S. 21st Division. From 1st December 1918 To 31st December 1918 Vol 39		
War Diary	Berlaimont	01/12/1918	14/12/1918
War Diary	Molliens-Vidame	15/12/1918	30/12/1918
Heading	War Diary of D.A.D.O.S. 21st Division. From 1st January 1919 To 31st January 1919 Vol 40		
War Diary	Molliens-Vidame	01/01/1919	30/01/1919
Heading	War Diary of D.A.D.O.S. 21st Division. From 1st February 1919 To 28th February, 1919 Vol 41		
War Diary	Molliens-Vidame	01/02/1919	03/03/1919
War Diary	Longpre	04/03/1919	31/05/1919

100.95/2140/2

21ST DIVISION

DEP. ASST DIR. ORDNANCE SERVICES

OCT 1915 - MAY 1919

Göttingen Stat. Str.
Bd: 1, 2, 3.

10/
794

Army Form W. 3091.

Cover for Documents.

Nature of Enclosures.

<u>Confidential.</u>

War Diary
of
D.A.D.O.S. 21st Division.

from 23/10/15 to 31/10/15

Notes, or Letters written.

WAR DIARY or INTELLIGENCE SUMMARY

Army Form C. 2118.

DADOS 21st Division.

Place	Date	Hour	Summary of Events and Information	Remarks and references to Appendices
MERRIS	23/10/15		I (Major A. Dymock AD.P. OO 3rd Class) took over duties of DADOS 21st Div" from Major Jindale ADP who had been acting as DADOS during the absence of Major Druk AD DADOS 21st Div" in Hospital. Visited STEENWERCK railhead of the Division. Ordinary routine work. Division is in Rest Billets. aD.	
MERRIS	24/10/15		Visited Corps Commander at BAILLEUL. DADOS of 25th & 50th Divisions also there. Corps Commander informed on us the necessity of avoiding "red tape" in connection with the supply of Shoes to Units. Usual routine work. aD	
MERRIS	25/10/15		At MERVILLE in connection with local purchase of bomb waistcoats for the Division. Issue of used P tube Smoke helmets, for instruction of troops in their use commenced. Usual routine work.	
MERRIS	26/10/15		At MERVILLE in connection with local purchase of bomb waistcoats. 50 Stoves Soyers received from Base - Divisional allowance for troops without other means of heating water. Usual routine work. aD.	
MERRIS	27/10/15		MAJOR BUSH discharged from hospital and returned to duty. 539 Magazines for Lewis Machine Guns received towards the 84 Per gun allowed. Jentbodmis commenced to arrive for tests in use with Division. aD.	

1875 Wt. W593/826 1,000,000 4/15 J.B.C. & A. A.D.S.S./Forms/C. 2118.

WAR DIARY
or
INTELLIGENCE SUMMARY

(Erase heading not required.)

Army Form C. 2118

Place	Date	Hour	Summary of Events and Information	Remarks and references to Appendices
MERRIS.	29/10/15		Received instructions to continue as DADOS 21st Div. MAJ. BUSH ordered to Calais. 01460 Sgt G. Crowther A.V.C. admitted to hospital 23rd inst. DDOS 2nd Army decided that Division DADsOS. Should hold a small stock of blankets in reserve to meet sudden requirements of reinforcements. 250 accordingly demanded from Base. Usual routine work. AD	
MERRIS	30/10/15		At PONT DE NIEPPE visiting DADsOS 50th Division re exchange of officers and Stores when 50th Div. move to MERRIS and 21st Div. to PONT DE NIEPPE which they are expected to do shortly. Usual routine work	
MERRIS.	30/10/15		At BAILLEUL purchasing 4 Vermoral Sprayers. Woollen drawers commenced from Base. Previously Base had issued cotton drawers in lieu of woollen on the Winter Scale with P.R.O. 1201. Usual routine work 13 Pistols Signal 1" received, first supply for Division. AD	
MERRIS	31/10/15		Visited 2nd Army workshops HAZEBROUCK and arranged to serve lorry weekly on Tuesdays to draw trench stores as they become available — trench Crothers Snipers copes Rifle Batteries Periscopes Scoops. &c. Usual routine work.	

A Dymock
Major
DADOS 21st Div

W 74—664 250,000 3/15 L.S.&Co.   Army Form W. 3091.

Cover for Documents.

Nature of Enclosures.

<u>Confidential.</u>

War diary
of
D.A.D.O.S. 21st Division.

from 1st Nov. 1915 to 30th Nov. 1915.

Notes, or Letters written.

Army Form C. 2118

D.A.D.O.S
21st Div.

WAR DIARY
or
INTELLIGENCE SUMMARY
(Erase heading not required.)

November 1915.

Instructions regarding War Diaries and Intelligence Summaries are contained in F. S. Regs., Part II. and the Staff Manual respectively. Title Pages will be prepared in manuscript.

Place	Date	Hour	Summary of Events and Information	Remarks and references to Appendices
MERRIS	1/11/15		Usual routine work. AD.	
MERRIS	2/11/15		Owing to units having duplicated indents for Lewis machine gun parts, magazines & the number "due out" at Base being obviously excessive, Base cancelled all demands. Units indents cancelled accordingly & units requested to indent for actual requirements. Instructions issued that units are to return all respirators as they have now been completed with helmets. Usual routine work. AD	
MERRIS	3/11/15		At Pont de Nieppe visiting D.A.D.O.S. 50th Div. in connection with exchange of shoes between the Divisions were. Three German shell had just landed behind his store. Sgt Payne A.O.C. (reverted from a Sgd Conductor when relieved by Sgt Crowter on 28/10/15) discharged from hospital. 104 Snipersopes (8 per battalion) received and issued under G.R.O. 1162 at MERVILLE to 676 bomb-waistcoats purchased and issued for Division. AD At BAILLEUL looking up local purchases. AD	
MERRIS	4/11/15			
MERRIS	5/11/15		Demanded Divisional allowance of braziers under G.R.O. 1209 from Base, also 180 tubs washing allowed for 10% of men in tents in winter AD.	

Army Form C. 2118

WAR DIARY
or
INTELLIGENCE SUMMARY

DADOS 21st Div. November 1915

(Erase heading not required.)

Place	Date	Hour	Summary of Events and Information	Remarks and references to Appendices
MERRIS	6/11/15		18316 goggles antigas, one for Officer and man of the Division demanded from Base. Usual routine work. aD	
MERRIS	7/11/15		Total dues out of binoculars prismatic are 148 including 14 for officers on present. Park of Machine Guns (Lewis) are to print at the Base that in demanding urgently a distinction has to be made between those to complete spares and those that are "unserviceable in the gun" ie the last spare but in gun + become unserviceable. Usual routine work. aD	
MERRIS	8/11/15		12 pistols signal 1st "received" making 25 in the Division. 100 Steel helmets received. Sgt PAYNE A.O.C. left the Division. Usual routine work aD	
PONT DE NIEPPE	9/11/15		Moved from MERRIS to PONT DE NIEPPE exchanging office of Store with DADOS 50th Division. Received instructions to demand Horseshoes frost cogs tips and wrenches for winter use from Base. Usual routine work. 95 & 96th Bdes RFA and A Bty 97th Bde RFA transferred 21st Div. from aD 50th Div. To Suffolk (Brigade Stores) and 1st NORTHUMBRIAN Bde. RFA from 21st to 50th Div.	
"	10/11/15		360 braziers received from Base. Usual routine work. aD	

Army Form C. 2118

WAR DIARY
or
INTELLIGENCE SUMMARY

DADOS "21st Div" November 1915.

Instructions regarding War Diaries and Intelligence Summaries are contained in F.S. Regs., Part II. and the Staff Manual respectively. Title Pages will be prepared in manuscript.

(Erase heading not required.)

Place	Date	Hour	Summary of Events and Information	Remarks and references to Appendices
PONT DE NIEPPE	11/11/15		Usual routine work. AD.	
—"—	12/11/15		HeadQuarters 21st Division moved from MERRIS to ARMENTIÈRES. Visited Head Quarters and arranged to visit them daily at 10 a.m. and 6 p.m. Pockets for smoke helmets cease to be supplied automatically with bulk supplies of Serwie Dress Jackets and are to be demanded as required in future. Usual routine work. AD.	
—"—	13/11/15		At BAILLEUL making local purchases. HeadQuarters 50th Division RE 1st NORTHUMBRIAN Field Coy. R.E. 2nd NORTHUMBRIAN Field Coy R.E. 7th Field Co. R.E. and 42nd ARMY TROOPS Coy. R.E transferred for supply of AOD stores from 50th Division to 21st Division. Usual routine work. AD.	
—"—	14/11/15		Usual routine work. AD.	
—"—	15/11/15		8th East YORKSHIRE Regt. and 12th WEST YORKSHIRE Regt. transferred to 3rd Division from 21st Division. 1st LINCOLN Regt and 4th MIDDLESEX Regt. transferred from 3rd Division to 21st Division.	

Army Form C. 21

D.A.D.O.S. 21st Div.n

WAR DIARY
or
INTELLIGENCE SUMMARY

(Erase heading not required.)

November 1915

Instructions regarding War Diaries and Intelligence Summaries are contained in F.S. Regs, Part II. and the Staff Manual respectively. Title Pages will be prepared in manuscript.

Place	Date	Hour	Summary of Events and Information	Remarks and references to Appendices
PONT DE NIEPPE	15/11/15		No 2. Mountain Battery transferred from 50th Div.n to 21st Div.n for supply of A.O.D. Stores. At BAILLEUL making local purchases. 14,000 goggles, antigas received from Base – First supply. 21st Divisional Armourers and Bootrepair Shops opened at PONT-DE NIEPPE, technically under me, otherwise under O.C. Salvage Coy. aD.	
"	16/11/15		"A" Squadron SOUTH IRISH HORSE and 65th FIELD AMBULANCE transferred for supply of Ordnance Stores from 21st to 50th Division. Making local purchases in ARMENTIÈRES. Usual routine work. aD.	
"	17/11/15		At CALAIS Army Ordnance Depôt and making local purchases there. aD	
"	18/11/15		First supplies of Jenkins leather received from Base (900) First 30 torches electric of 200 due to Headquarters of the Division, received from Base. Usual routine work. aD	
"	19/11/15		259 magazines for Lewis Machine Guns received from Base, also first supply of Horse Shoes prepaid for Corps, and first Cargs. Usual routine work. aD.	

Army Form C. 2118

D.A.D.O.S. 21st Divn.

WAR DIARY
or
INTELLIGENCE SUMMARY

November 1915.

Place	Date	Hour	Summary of Events and Information	Remarks and references to Appendices
PONT DE NIEPPE	20/11/15		4000 goggles antigas received from Base. 2nd Blanket per man received. 50 Steel helmets received from Base. At BAILLEUL making local purchases. Usual routine work.	
—"—	21/11/15		837 Magazines for Lewis Machine Guns received making 1096 to date. Usual routine work.	
—"—	22/11/15		43 rifles with telescope sights due to Division only 9 having been received so far. 316 goggles antigas received, completing requirements of the Division. 4550 Blankets received from Base towards three Blankets as 2nd line per man — first supply. 200 Lanterns Ford folding received from Base Completing the 250 allowed to the Division. Usual routine work.	
—"—	23/11/15			
—"—	24/11/15		Owing to scarcity of undercoats fur and Jerkins leather at Base issue restricted for the present to men in trenches, Gun detachments Motor Cyclists &c. Divisional allowance of 208 bulged rifles to fire rifle grenades completed, the rifles having been collected from Armourers Shops of 6th and 14th Divisions. Indents for second "P." tube Smoke helmet per man, called for and demand made on Base for 18800.	

Army Form C. 2118

WAR DIARY
or
INTELLIGENCE SUMMARY
(Erase heading not required.)

S.A.D.S. 21st Div.

November 1915.

Instructions regarding War Diaries and Intelligence
Summaries are contained in F.S. Regs., Part II.
and the Staff Manual respectively. Title Pages
will be prepared in manuscript.

Place	Date	Hour	Summary of Events and Information	Remarks and references to Appendices
PONT DE NIEPPE	25/11/15		Usual routine work. A.D.	
— " —	26/11/15		100 Steel helmets received from Base. Instructions received that owing to scarcity of Vests Woollen, Shirts flannel may be demanded in lieu. Usual routine work. A.D.	
— " —	27/11/15		1st EAST YORKSHIRE Reg.t transferred from 6th Division to 21st Division. 14th DURHAM LIGHT INFANTRY transferred from 21st Division to 6th Division. A.o.C. 02902 Pte R. OWEN admitted to hospital. Usual routine work. A.D.	
— " —	28/11/15		Lewis machine gun received for 63rd Bde. Usual routine work. A.D.	
— " —	29/11/15		50 torches electric received for Headquarters of the Division & 250 Magazines for Lewis machine guns received from Base. Usual routine work.	
— " —	30/11/15		Usual routine work.	

A.D.S. work
Major
S.A.D.S. 21st Div.n

W 74—664 250,000 3/15 L.S. & Co.   Army Form W. 3091.

Cover for Documents.

Nature of Enclosures.

Confidential.

War Diary
of
D.A.D.O.S. 21st Division.

from 1/12/15 to 19/12/15.

Notes, or Letters written.

WAR DIARY

D.A.D.O.T. 21st Divn INTELLIGENCE SUMMARY December 1915

Place	Date	Hour	Summary of Events and Information	Remarks and references to Appendices
PONT DE NIEPPE	1/12/15		At A.O.D. workshop, 5th Corps STEENVOORDE for No. 7 Dial Sight for 18/pr. gun "B" Battery 94th Bde. R.F.A. out of action. Also at CASSEL seeing D.D.O.S. 2nd Army on various questions. Usual routine work. a.D.	
"	2/12/15		At BAILLEUL making local purchases. Usual routine work. a.D.	
"	3/12/15		Sergt CROWTER A.O.C. made a/Sub. Conductor dating from 15/11/15. Owing to scarcity of jackets, cardigan instructions received to check indents with Speed card and report weekly to D.D.O.S. 2nd Army the number demanded from Base. Usual routine work. a.D.	
"	4/12/15		Shells falling near PONT DE NIEPPE. Usual routine work a.D.	
"	5/12/15		Usual routine work. a.D.	
"	6/12/15		50 Steel helmets received. Patches and solution for it an of Gumboots received. It has been arranged that the Divisional Boot Repair Shop will patch gumboots and when vulcanising is necessary obtain services of vulcanizer from Supply Column or Divisional Ambulance Workshops. At BAILLEUL making local purchases a.D.	

Army Form C. 2118

WAR DIARY
or
INTELLIGENCE SUMMARY

(Erase heading not required.)

D.A.D.O.S. 51st Div"   December 1915.

Place	Date	Hour	Summary of Events and Information	Remarks and references to Appendices
PONT DE NIEPPE	7/12/15		Headquarters 50th Division R.E. 1/1 and 1/2 NORTHUMBERLAND FIELD Companies R.E. and 7th FIELD Company R.E. re-transferred to 50th Division for supply of Ordnance Stores. Pte OWEN A.O.C. discharged from hospital. At BAILLEUL working local purchases. A.D.	
"	8/12/15		Usual routine work. A.D.	
"	9/12/15		No 2 MOUNTAIN Battery transferred to 2nd Army Troops for supply of Ordnance Stores. 100 Steel helmets received at BAILLEUL re material for haillasses for the purchase of which £100 has been allowed. Shell falling near PONT DE NIEPPE A.D.	
"	10/12/15		213 magazines for Lewis Machine Guns received at Railhead, and at HAZEBROUCK re material for haillasses. Usual routine work A.D.	
"	11/12/15		At MERVILLE re local purchase of nosebags and cooks' overalls. Bulk supplies of horseshoes from Base very short almost and have been short for some weeks.	

Army Form C. 2118

D.A.D.O.S 21st Divn

WAR DIARY
or
INTELLIGENCE SUMMARY

(Erase heading not required.)

December 1915

Instructions regarding War Diaries and Intelligence Summaries are contained in F.S. Regs., Part II. and the Staff Manual respectively. Title Pages will be prepared in manuscript.

Place	Date	Hour	Summary of Events and Information	Remarks and references to Appendices
PONT DE NIEPPE	11/12/15		Demanded 12 Lewis machine guns from Base to complete Division with Lewis guns and release Vickers and Maxims for Bde Machine Gun Companies which are being formed. a.D.	
"	12/12/15		"D" Battery 97th Bde. R.F.A. transferred from 21st Division to 2nd Canadian Division for supply of Ordnance Stores. At MERVILLE re purchase of short waistcoats. Supplies of pantaloons from Base short at present. Commenced local purchase locally and issuing to troops clothes brushes for removing mud from their uniforms. a.D.	
"	13/12/15		At MERVILLE re local purchases. Usual routine work. a.D.	
"	14/12/15		At CALAIS by car for 3 cylinders gas for Lewis machine guns for 63rd Infantry Bde. to replace others which had become unserviceable and put the guns out of action, there being no stores available. a.D.	
"	15/12/15		At MERVILLE re local purchase of nosebags and cooks' overalls. 50 stud helmets received.	

Army Form C. 2113

D.A.D.O.S. 21st Div"

WAR DIARY
or
INTELLIGENCE SUMMARY
(Erase heading not required.)

December 1915.

Place	Date	Hour	Summary of Events and Information	Remarks and references to Appendices
PONT DE NIEPPE	16/12/15		Received instructions to visit D.D.O.S. 2nd Army at CASSEL. Did so and was informed that I had been appointed A.D.O.S. 2nd Corps.	
"	17/12/15		Major WILLIAMS-FREEMAN A.O.D. arrived to take over duties of D.A.D.O.S. 21st Division. Temporary LIEUT. QUARRIE A.O.D arrived for instruction in duties of D.A.D.O.S. At BAILLEUL and MERVILLE re local purchases. Usual routine work.	
"	18/12/15		Usual routine work and handing over to Major WILLIAMS-FREEMAN A.D	
"	19/12/15		Completed handing over to Major WILLIAMS-FREEMAN and left for BAILLEUL to take up duties of A.D.O.S. 2nd Corps.	

A Dymock
Lt Col. A.O.D.

Extra. 21st Dir.
part of Vol: 3
D Dec 1915.

Confidential

War Diary
of
D.A.D.S. 21st Division

from Dec: 18th 1915 to Dec: 31st 1915

L Williams-Freeman Major
DADS 21' Div.

Army Form C. 2118.

WAR DIARY
or
~~INTELLIGENCE SUMMARY~~
(Erase heading not required.)

Place	Date	Hour	Summary of Events and Information	Remarks and references to Appendices
Armentières	19/15 etc. 18.		Commenced taking over. I find the division is not now in the British system for Ordnance supplies. I think I shall probably change the system. Lieut Ausonie arrived to undergo a months instruction in duties of S.D.S.S. AWR	
"	19		Completed taking over & began synged left to take up duties of A.D.B.S. 2nd Corps. My office here is about a mile from the Div. which is a disadvantage as I only go at the end of a day. Much better to run one office near D. Train so as to be able to consult them of one on any question that arises. I am also moving with the Hd. Qrs. of the Train – another disadvantage as one does not get to know the staff with whom one is brought into contact for official purposes. AWR	
"	21.		Visited Bailleul Hazebrouck and Merville for local purchases. AWR	

Army Form C. 2118.

WAR DIARY
or
INTELLIGENCE SUMMARY.
(Erase heading not required.)

Place	Date	Hour	Summary of Events and Information	Remarks and references to Appendices
Armentieres	1915 Ju. 22.		Visited A.D.S.S. 2nd Army & discussed several questions with him. It seems that L'Heuraie is to take over from me when reported ready to do so. AWF	
"	23		Saw the O.C. A/95 R.F.A. & O.C. 95th B.A.C. & discussed with them the position of gun stores. Colonel Symonds - A.D.S. S"Corps - c/10 called & went into several questions. Lewis guns are giving trouble dead frank through brickdust, & misfired. I am repairing pistons rods of the guns as now been notified & I am waiting for a report as to whether they are satisfactory. AWF	
"	24.		Went to Bailleul for torch purchases. Also visited Railhead, Great stores & Horse Show Gain this week from Base. Reported to A.D.S. 2nd Army. AWF.	
"	25.		Proceeded to 14th stn. Found they had just received orders cancelling	

Army Form C. 2118.

WAR DIARY
or
INTELLIGENCE SUMMARY.
(Erase heading not required.)

Instructions regarding War Diaries and Intelligence Summaries are contained in F. S. Regs., Part II. and the Staff Manual respectively. Title pages will be prepared in manuscript.

Place	Date	Hour	Summary of Events and Information	Remarks and references to Appendices
	1915			
	Dec.		Hein morr. AWR.	
Armentières	26		Saw Staff Captain R.A. & Lt. Col. to G. Both seem fairly satisfied as regards Ordnance Supplies. AWR	
"	27		Visited A.D.O.S. 2nd Army who confirmed that I should to Leave this Division but could give me no information as to my destination. I trust it is not to be the Base. Made some Local purchases on way back. AWR	
"	28am		Visited Armourers Shop, Salvage Company and Field Ambce Workshop. The Latter unit is undertaking repairs to Piston rods of Lewis Guns. Had a fied sight repaired in Bailleul. AWR	
"	29		Visited to introduce the British system I controlling visiting Between Stores. I featured the W.O's who are to take charge of Brigades in this	

Army Form C. 2118.

WAR DIARY
~~INTELLIGENCE~~ SUMMARY
(Erase heading not required.)

Place	Date	Hour	Summary of Events and Information	Remarks and references to Appendices
Armentières	1918 Dec. 29		Dentist. The system will take a little time before it works smoothly and I am a little doubtful of the man I have put in charge. I finished visiting Troops. He is not very bright in my opinion but has been recommended for promotion to Sergeant by a former S.A.D.V.S. Div?	
"	31		Supply of Horse & Mule Shoes extremely bad. It has been getting worse every week for the past month or six weeks. Glanders put this unit to 2nd Group. I understand the A.D.V.S. is also taking the matter up. ADV?	

A. Williams
Lieut Veg?
A.D.V.S. 21st Div.

O/c A&R Section

Can you kindly say to which unit the attached War Diary belongs

[signature]
D.A.A.G.1

22.2.16

CONFIDENTIAL

A.G.'s OFFICE AT THE BASE
CENTRAL REGISTRY
23 FEB 1916
C.R. No. 140/914.

PTO

CONFIDENTIAL

D.A.Q.1.

From 1–7/16:
Major A Williams-Freeman
D.A.D.O.S.
1st. Division.

8–31/16
T. Lieut R S Quarrie
D.A.D.O.S.
1st. Division

Lieut-Colonel,
Officer i/c Army Ordnance Corps, Records,
3rd Echelon, British Exped. Force.

25 FEB. 1916

Army Form C. 2118.

WAR DIARY

(Erase heading not required.)

Place	Date	Hour	Summary of Events and Information	Remarks and references to Appendices
Armentières	1916 Jany 1st		A further supply of Horse Shoes arrived to-day which makes the position c. Little better, but still the position re: the reviews. AuR	
"	2nd		Tudor Lewis Guns arrived. This completes the division to four Guns per Infantry Battalion. Consequently Tudor Vickers & Maxim Guns are released. These are to be with-drawn but without Transport to 3rd and 6th divisions. Arranged accordingly with the H.Q. Res. AuR.	
	4th		Proceeded to Merville for Local purchases. AuR	
	5th		Notified that 2500 pairs of Gum Boots Thigh will shortly be issued to division. AuR	
	6th		Received orders to proceed to Havre for duty. Shall leave on 8th AuR	
	7		Handed over to L' Guerrie AuR	

WAR DIARY or INTELLIGENCE SUMMARY

Army Form C. 2118

Place	Date	Hour	Summary of Events and Information	Remarks and references to Appendices
Pnt de hippe	8/1/16		Major Williams-Freeman leaves for Havre to report then for duty.	
"	9/-		Visited 2nd Army workshops + enquired from Q. Grey [?] (50) back 2500 pairs of Gum Boots that received and issued to Infantry Brigades. Viewed deaf heaters RA + also H.Q. of the 3 Infantry Brigades. All seem satisfied with Greener service generally.	
"	10/-		Visited Sir Cutler (40) + manufacturing material destined to Calais. Rate to get from Ingrasut Calais re thing of handles of same. Questioning of Lewis Gun Parts. Matter is being enquired into.	
"	11/-		Arranged for inauguration of 200 new Ps/Boys at huvier.	
"	12/-		Routine duties. B.E. Duke Train reports Thunderman Boots needed	
"	13/-		too perfect organisal and purposes of Gym & further purchase of temps up to the £100 each	
"	14/-		Routine duties.	

Army Form C. 2118

WAR DIARY
or
INTELLIGENCE SUMMARY
(Erase heading not required.)

Instructions regarding War Diaries and Intelligence Summaries are contained in F.S. Regs., Part II. and the Staff Manual respectively. Title Pages will be prepared in manuscript.

Place	Date	Hour	Summary of Events and Information	Remarks and references to Appendices
Pont-de-hippe	15/4/16.		Visited howitzers for Gen Forestier. 200 hrs. Bags & now howitzer lamps. Was unable to go further, given for Forestier so the Car was not available until the afternoon. Mentioned this at Headquarters. Shortage of 5.0 hrs. Bags in to-days Bulk Stores. (Motor duties).	
"	16/-			
"	17/-		Visited howitzers and Haycoreer & pleased men for 300 hrs Aug 16 & men about shortage. holpen that units are to be supplied to Div. Own about shortage. hopes that units are to be supplied to Div. in sufficient numbers to enable every man to have a clean on Baths in different humbers to enable every man to have a clean on Baths. Interviewed O/C (Stay requesting this when he visits the Baths. Major Tisdale (2nd Army) visited this office and Major Austin the Ordnance generally and the equipment Discussion re Ordnance in Section in Contenen.	
"	18/-		of Machine Gun Section in Contenen.	
"	19/-		6 Three Guns (18 (?)) of a Battery had nil of action. Special Trench Storge Run. Twin Hebron for Artillery expended. noted fn 360.	

WAR DIARY
or
INTELLIGENCE SUMMARY
(Erase heading not required.)

Army Form C. 2118

Place	Date	Hour	Summary of Events and Information	Remarks and references to Appendices
Prii-au-hippe	20/9/16.		Local Issues of Note Bags and Lamps Invisible at Hyperneck and howitzer. No more Tubes Helmets to be issued to Hyperneck as they are now being supplied with them at the Base. Return duplic.	
"	21/-			
"	22/-		Big demand for S. Guns Seeping an making endeavours to procure locally. Visited 2nd Army Workshops at Hazebrouck in hopes Fuze for Div. 9 B.L. was made to obtain them.	
"	23/-		Arranged with I.O.M. 2nd Corps to exchange serviceable Guns — one of the them rendered unserviceable by Enemy's Shellfire — for me of them references from Base.	
"	24/-		Respirators to be provided with P.H. Tube Pattern Helmet and "P" Tube Pat. released to be sent to Base. 5000 "P Tube" Pat. being held as a Divisional Reserve. Two Ptes. of appearance for Duty have arrived for Traing. ("U" Blankets) for Duty as a Curtain in case of gas attack.	
"	25/-		Discussion re Using	

WAR DIARY or INTELLIGENCE SUMMARY

Army Form C. 2118

Place	Date	Hour	Summary of Events and Information	Remarks and references to Appendices
26th Jan/'15. Pont de Nieppe			Arranged with "Q" to have a return from units of all tents in their possession and whether necessary. Position regarding Rest Huts in Lain Quay site very unsatisfactory. Seems essential to have a bigger reserve of this than 1 per Gun.	
"	27		Sent 14 trappers (to allowance of 1 torpedo per 2 Guns) Torpedoes back to units. It was noted arrival of Brigade M.G. Coy from the Div. "Q". Action was taken in writing same from Custom for expenses Gun Boots arrival; also 800 patches from Boulogne for repair of Gum Boots. Handed him over 16 Brotheshoes Shop & repairs on hand presently.	
"	28		Have method of having Gas Helmets for service (to be dropped immediately they had ready) the arrival of new gas Helmets to replace these when necessary. Under this scheme never only about Three days apart from any gas attack & he then to be replaced. The wastage for week for the Division will no be approximately 1800 Helmets in a gas a gas arrival.	
"	29			

Army Form C. 2118

WAR DIARY
or
INTELLIGENCE SUMMARY
(Erase heading not required.)

Place	Date	Hour	Summary of Events and Information	Remarks and references to Appendices
Pont du Hem	30/1/15		2nd Army order That no more Bicycles Folding are to be manufactured. Only 4 at present in Th Division.	
"	31/1/15		Arranged with Headquarters & O.C. Salvage Coy. respecting return to Base of "P Tube Helmets" on being replaced by "Hexamine" helmets.	

R. Guerin Lieut. A.D.P.

SADop. 21ᵗ Div:
Vol: 5

Army Form C. 2118

WAR DIARY
or
INTELLIGENCE SUMMARY
(Erase heading not required.)

Instructions regarding War Diaries and Intelligence Summaries are contained in F.S. Regs., Part II. and the Staff Manual respectively. Title Pages will be prepared in manuscript.

Place	Date	Hour	Summary of Events and Information	Remarks and references to Appendices
Armentières	1/2/16		Only Two Batteries (R.F.A.) in Division Complete with Perfecting Spring Gear. Been urged on for this. Lines continue both.	
"	2/-	-	Endeavouring so far no promise to have small repairs to Magn Wheels & Carriel as Beset. Heyfore repairs carried out cheaply & efficiently at Divisional Armouries. Known to been for 2/Lt. P.H. Tuck. Helmet pen A.E. Chains.	
"	3/-	-	Routine work.	
"	4/-	-	View L.T.R. of apparatus for turning Lovis Barrels undergoing Trial in R. Dinas. Has arranged for Guns (spt. repairmen tools to be made in the Div. of Div. FMB. Workspace)	
"	5/-	-	Division seems overissed equipped with small armaments generally. Extra 300 bayonets + Butt. F.P. rifles will have been recalled at Basil.	
"	6/-	-	Visited 2 Army Troops & collected 5 French Periscopes (2 by J. & 3 Artillery)	
"	7/-	-	Division has equipped to 1 per all ranks with P.H. Smoke Helmet P. No special Goggle Type helmets for Artillery (P.H.) received yet.	
"	8/-	-	Arranged with Heady masters for 1 man from Brigade to view 2nd/ Corps Workshop for a Return in Vermorel Sprayers - workshops and repair.	

WAR DIARY
or
INTELLIGENCE SUMMARY

(Erase heading not required.)

Army Form C. 2118

Place	Date	Hour	Summary of Events and Information	Remarks and references to Appendices
Pt. ou. hippos	9th Feby '16		A further allowance of $100 to Divan for Coster Iwarks has been made. Steem order for 334 I.o. days	
"	10		Obtained permission from Divi Headquarters to experiment with a new method of repairing Pain Roods for Four Guns. Had 3 made to my sketch & proved to Brigadier. Reports very satisfactory.	
"	11		Made arrangements with Headquarters and O.C. Salvage Coy. to have all unprepared Anke Boots and Gun Boots given over to me to meet absolute min. Whilst in elimination of demands on Base — By me and is found to procure between 90 Division had been Government. His seen that surplus the wooden huts & Build and 100 Bell Tents manhunged. Two tents are to spared.	
"	12		To replace tents only tents can be spared. Lusha Hakamat & arrived today. 14 Stated driven 18,900 feet Pitt pati. ½" Brigade to 2 pm Ghen theal. P Two Boot Helmets	
"	13		A further 1 Pan Guns from is (no equipment) to 1 Pan from from to Bear slowly. Being withdrawn to Base slowly. Prestri Austria	
"	14		Commenced overpatching & template of 198 Teri Bothern to Base. Then were exp by the Div to 7 Div. a leaving that R Retrn.	
"	15		in the forenoon of this Div.	

WAR DIARY or INTELLIGENCE SUMMARY

Army Form C. 2118

Place	Date	Hour	Summary of Events and Information	Remarks and references to Appendices
Pont du Nieppe	16/2/16	—	Trench Outfits.	
"	17/-	—	Division is equipped to 2 per all ranks with Pt. Helmets. P.T.U. Patter. Being steadily returned to Base about 15000 so far returned.	
"	18/-	—	6 "Strombos" horns for Gas Alarms now in Division being experimented with.	
"	19/-	—	Routine duties.	
"	20/-	—	"	
"	21/-	—	Divisional Battery has returned all repairs. Batt. R.E. try & stop for division. This matter leaves any chance of Enemy seeing the Craters are to U.vision by any inf. preparing the Fastener edge. Trusted that they can be seen by any inf. preparing to day.	
"	22/-	—	24 hrs. Protective Germ Case received to-day. Pistol Rods for Lewis Machine Guns — repairs to these on us being carried out meeting half of run of... of plug stock. I have had much difficulty in being retained for this unit till such time as some decision has been arrived at in the proposed... government a fortnight ago.	

Army Form C. 2118

WAR DIARY
or
INTELLIGENCE SUMMARY
(Erase heading not required.)

Instructions regarding War Diaries and Intelligence Summaries are contained in F.S. Regs., Part II. and the Staff Manual respectively. Title Pages will be prepared in manuscript.

Place	Date	Hour	Summary of Events and Information	Remarks and references to Appendices
Pont du Hem	23/2/16		Receiving instructions in main Bedf info cent. Hereby arrangements with incoming Division re Divisional stores.	
"	24/		Revised scale of heliographs — see enquiry to Hrs being returned to Base. Routine duties.	
"	25/			
"	26/		Returns of Trench Stores &c to Divl. Q. shew considerable discrepancies in almost every case. Given the shortfall/recent issues to this Division and the fact which this Division was equipped with troops in trenches + in Billets. Being made at Divisional Q. it appears they are being serviced by the enquiry being made in further unjustifiable & perhaps extremely slow on the Staff Officer concerned.	
"	27/		Chief Staff Authorities. Reporting to HQ Corps.	
"	28/		Charge wrote the Provost Marshal Genl. Carrier (hand). Injuries have been made up to him asking for Systems of Corps which has been taken to every charging over the Enemy Trenches & being connumerd. together with better system of Defence.	
"	29/			

R.A. Quinnin Lieut.
D.A.D.O.S. 21st DIVISION.

A.S. A. 7 A. 21 Vol 6/

WAR DIARY
or
INTELLIGENCE SUMMARY

(Erase heading not required.)

Army Form C. 2118

Place	Date	Hour	Summary of Events and Information	Remarks and references to Appendices
Port de Hesdin	1/3/16		Tactical exercise	
"	2/-		Lieut. R.S. Murray reported here for a period of instruction as a D.O.O.	
"	3/-		150 Box Respirators "Ship Outs" received from Corps. 50 gns. to each Infantry Bde. These are to be used as a curtain to protect Dug Outs in case of Gas Attack. Drop front overnight to allow from units for photo kim.	
"	4/-		2 m/ Leather Helmet par us raised approved. Div. I.O. Saw for 19000 Helmets & Satchels.	
"	5/-			
"	6/-		The present system of dealing with Rifles fitted with Telescopic Sights dinned down unsatisfactory as the Rifles Sometimes used Anyway Sent for this weeks without being used. Have requested this matter to A.D.O.S. 2nd Corps.	
"	7/-		There are now 4/3 Divisions drawn for Gas Alarm to this Division. Machine Gun Companies arrived yesterday. Units have as been desired to return the March IV Tripod mountings which have been returned until arrival of Machine Gun Company.	

WAR DIARY
or
INTELLIGENCE SUMMARY

Army Form C. 2118

(Erase heading not required.)

Place	Date	Hour	Summary of Events and Information	Remarks and references to Appendices
Port-de-hicsape	8/3/16		Had great trouble in finding any information respecting location of 182 Tunnelling Coy. Divisional 'Q' had had no information on the subject. Question of the returning winter clothing has been referred to this formation for settlement. Am arranging with Salvage Coy. to find a class steel store can be improvised for small items allotted to us by Army.	
	9/-			
	10/-		Visited the 177th Division with a view to changing over stores when possible.	
	11/-			
	12/-		Visited the 17th Division with a view to changing over stores when possible.	
	13/-			
	14/-		It has been decided to effect an exchange of Guns between the Artillery of the Div. (17th & 21st). At present the preferred is to hand over the Gun and Carriage only. The spares in the carriage will also be handed over. (Also to 7. See Reft of Comm.) The spares with the C.R.A. for the new equipment taken over by this Division to be armoured for a list of deficiencies free Battery to the nearest to any to be immediately minimum on a similar with be arrived off. The remainder of spare. Any items which are already in Indents be cancelled. This will avoid any cancellation of Indents at Base.	

Army Form C. 2118

WAR DIARY
or
INTELLIGENCE SUMMARY
(Erase heading not required.)

Instructions regarding War Diaries and Intelligence Summaries are contained in F. S. Regs., Part II. and the Staff Manual respectively. Title Pages will be prepared in manuscript.

Place	Date	Hour	Summary of Events and Information	Remarks and references to Appendices
Pont-de-Nieppe	15/3/16		Pieces of work have been discovered in trenches. Those nearly do have in this. This has been carried out at the Baths. It is hoped their this practice will better be carried out at the Baths. In the meantime units are warning their statement to exercise greater care making up their fours.	
	16/1/-			
	17/1/-		The move back to front area of this Div. after being in the trenches all winter must have had a rejuvenating for the winter clothing of the other units has been issued during the period noted.	
	18/1/-			
	19/1/-		Routine duties.	
	20/1/-		Routine duties. Col. Ama of Lewis Guns referred with the new form of play but one of the Pistol Ames to his facility Col. + they have taken in hand for nearly two militia. Intervals by me to be + hitting for 16-minutes notice to theorin.	
	21/1/-		Routine duties and preparation for thuris at 9 a.m. Left Pont-de-Nieppe for thuris at 9 a.m.	

WAR DIARY
or
INTELLIGENCE SUMMARY
(Erase heading not required.)

Army Form C. 2118

Place	Date	Hour	Summary of Events and Information	Remarks and references to Appendices
Mersa	22/3/16	—	In view of an early move of Division to 4th Army it has been decided to get in Green Winter Clothing - Leather Jerkins, Undercoats, Furs and Horse Rugs.	
"	23/-	—	Corps arranging transport for this Division at Railhead.	
"	24/-	—	Advance Guard Train has no further issue to this Division after 24% (Train Advance Guard Train has no further issue to this Div. after 24% (Train also advised similarly). That was also because in anticipated moving South in F.E. 27? by units. Approximate	
"	25/-	—	very few percentage of Horses & Horse Rugs have been returned by many units as the Division had not been warned. Horse Rugs have been retained by many units as they would be sorry to part with them yet. 257% of Horse Rugs have been retained by many units and the A.D.V.S. considered it would be sorry to part with them yet.	
"	26/-	—	Extra 2 (Two) Vickers Guns per Infantry Battalion arrived to day (26 in all.) Lance Corp. Carter left to day for transport duty with 2nd Army D.D.O.S. He has been attached to in Brief the 18th February for a course of instruction in the duties of a Brigade Warrant Officer.	
"	27/-	—	Date of move of this department has been postponed until the 30/7.	

WAR DIARY
or
INTELLIGENCE SUMMARY

(Erase heading not required.)

Army Form C. 2118

Place	Date	Hour	Summary of Events and Information	Remarks and references to Appendices
Mesnil	28/3/16		Cleaning up trenches as in anticipation of move.	
"	29/-			
"	30/-		Was unable to obtain a car to move with my Tyn Cwms so travelled with Hd. Army to Jauvillay Hanaulo in m. of Tyn Cwms and latter the after midday & got in South Nch Am. At Aire in the Tyn Tnde neuenhdin a visit to the Tyn Tnds at Isbergue Steel Works. 91 am moved again in C.T. Cars and 7pm when in movement lauren tu hnies notwith [thuing] the night.	
	31/-		For the past fortnight I have been senouly handicapped in my work owing to not being able to get a car. All the headquarter cars are fully employed in this division and the arrangement is not satisfactory from my point of view.	

T.B. Iuvris Capt.
D.A.C.C.S.
21st DIVISION.

D.A.G.
3rd Echelon

Herewith War Diary for the Two (2) months April and May 1916.

As I was absent on leave at the end of April my Diary for that month was not sent forward so I decided to send the Two Together.

I hope this is in order.

Asmarin Capt
DADTT 2, DIV
Headquarters.

11/6/16

Army Form C. 2118

DADOS 21 / 3
Vol 7. 8

WAR DIARY or INTELLIGENCE SUMMARY
(Erase heading not required.)

Place	Date	Hour	Summary of Events and Information	Remarks and references to Appendices
Rouen	1/4/16		Arrived here at 10-30 a.m. having spent two days on the journey from Marseilles. On 31st the train broke down twice. The train chosen for me by Divl Headquarters was thirty minutes, so I arranged 176 train another train. As explained in last month's diary there were 10 Prisoners on to run down to the area before the Division moved.	
"	2/-		Visited R.O.D. & discussed the question of the return of winter clothing &c stores on this Division. The Ordnance Ship has been sunk — except from Technical Supervision.	
"	3/-		By the Salvage Coy, have arranged for them to be stored under my charge.	
"	4/-		Stores have not yet been received from the store though they were unloaded from the ship 2/4/16. They now are arriving & should be in readiness to receive them in the further train when it arrives here.	
"	5-4-16		Programme showing dates of despatch of winter clothing & Some Drs HQ. Circulated a letter trade units in Subject. Received.	
"	6 4 16		Provision made for cats return on 15th April, to Brigades & received letter to be returned on 15th April.	
"	7-4-16		000 French Helmets received for Infantry Brigs. Instructions received that all N.C.Os Personages received, showed be reports to H.Q. XIII Corps who whitled give orders as to disposal.	

Army Form C. 2118

WAR DIARY
or
INTELLIGENCE SUMMARY
(Erase heading not required.)

Instructions regarding War Diaries and Intelligence Summaries are contained in F. S. Regs., Part II. and the Staff Manual respectively. Title Pages will be prepared in manuscript.

Place	Date	Hour	Summary of Events and Information	Remarks and references to Appendices
Réberrant	8/9/16		1,638 Steel Helmets received from 15th Division.	
—	9/9/16		Routine work	
—	10/9/16		Indents received from Town kept for now supplying tobr. & Provented to.	
—	11/9/16		Above received & prepared & 9 Cases French Horizon Cloth. These were not delivered to the Division but sent direct to 7th M. School under orders of 77Q Fourth Army.	
—	12/9/16		Two stores with flat-rood purchased for Bde Baths to enable men's Clo. to be ironed.	
—	13/9/16		Routine work. Indent for 18,445 P.H. helmets submitted to replace 5000 P P Helmets held as Reserve.	
—	14/9/16		Information received the 'D' Batter 97th Bde. detaches whilst in II Corps has left the Distr. + the Horritzer Brigade now becomes a 3 Butty Bde.	
—	15/9/16		400 Steel Helmets received from Base.	
—	16/9/16		Routine work.	

1875 Wt. W593/826 1,000,000 4/15 J.B.C. & A. A.D.S.S./Forms/C. 2118.

Army Form C. 2118

WAR DIARY
or
INTELLIGENCE SUMMARY
(Erase heading not required.)

Place	Date	Hour	Summary of Events and Information	Remarks and references to Appendices
Ribemont	17/7/16		12,444 P.H. Helmets to Reserve Reserves from Base. 5000 P Pattern despatched to Base. 120 Blankets for use in dug-outs appropriated from those returned by Troops	
—	18/7/16		12 good containers received from XIII Corps. 5705 P.H. Helmets received from Abbeville to complete Reserve 1/1 per officer & man.	
—	19/7/16		Return forwarded.	
—	20/7/16		Indent forwarded to Base for 2229 Box Respirators in accordance with 49 Army Order.	
—	21/7/16		170 tents C.S.L. wounded for in accordance with Corps letter 932/14.	
—	22/7/16		Arrangements have been made with Base to supply Army's for Steel Helmets to The Divisional Ammunition Column supply the same.	
—	23/7/16		Rangers with	
—	24/7/16		26 Lewis M.Guns received making 8 per Battalion.	

WAR DIARY
or
INTELLIGENCE SUMMARY

Army Form C. 2118

(Erase heading not required.)

Place	Date	Hour	Summary of Events and Information	Remarks and references to Appendices
Rilé...	25/4/16		No stores received from Base. Purchased 20 kilos of paint under urgent orders received from 8th Bn. HQ for use on B200 Bdy. Telegram received in respect postcard. One Tobacco Garrison received from OO XIII Corps Troops.	
—	26.4.16		Good supply of Boots antle received from Base. Purchased Paint for "Stokes" 94th Bde. For use in guns in exposed position. Brought to notice of O Branch 21 Div. that excessive N° of Boots issued to 9th KOYLI since 1-1-16. Ordered from Louis Grenade.	
—	27.4.16		100 Vermorel Sprayers received. Reg. for Carriage of field. Arrived R.B.W. XIII Corps Q.C. 264/2 2-96/4 4-21-4-16. — delivery within a week. Routine work.	
—	28.4.16		Attention to Shell panels (additional panels to be added) but we have at arrival. Office — dump visited by appr. XIII Corps.	appx 13
—	29.4.16		Office — dump visited by Brig General M.G.E. Barton CB CMG DSO. unloading of truck at Railhead did not commence. 200 steel helmets received. also 700 gun goggles unknown.	

Routine Work.

WAR DIARY or INTELLIGENCE SUMMARY

Army Form C. 2118

Place	Date	Hour	Summary of Events and Information	Remarks and references to Appendices
Ritemont	30-4-16		No stores received from Base. Routine work.	Copy PIV OAP8 21 30.4.16
"	1-5-16	1.30 a.m.	Urgent orders received to issue to 6/39 Bn. 50 Vermorel sprayers and 50 Vermorel sprayers from reserve which should have been completed by 1.45 a.m. 1000 Steel helmets received.	
"	1.5.16		2 Trucks of Stores which were not ready for unloading in 4 hrs. were in position at 8 a.m. The trucks were in a central line & more-or-less had to recoile the stores re caunies across another set of metals to the plates - the plates re caunies across another set of metals caused. Take location into lorries. Question of inconvenience resulting. O.C. VIII Corps Railhead who has been asked to arrange upwards ROD VIII Corps Railhead to undertake movement to a suitable position for trucks to Helmets P.H. issue to replace a similar hour. 1960 'Reserve' smoke Bde Pri: 10 pr Q × 969 to replace smoke after the gas attack of 30.4.16. b/20/3/de HQrs Vide Pri: 10 pr Q × 969 for use after the gas attack of 30.4.16. number rendered unsafe for use. Tents received to supplement billeting accommodation.	
"	2-5-16		170 Oth Tents received to supplement billeting accommodation. All units C⁰: - 13"Blanket received + drawn from Complete. Routine work.	
"	3-5-16		900 Steel helmets received from Base. 170 ors required. received from 13th Bn.	

Army Form C. 2118

WAR DIARY
or
INTELLIGENCE SUMMARY
(Erase heading not required.)

Instructions regarding War Diaries and Intelligence Summaries are contained in F. S. Regs., Part II. and the Staff Manual respectively. Title Pages will be prepared in manuscript.

Place	Date	Hour	Summary of Events and Information	Remarks and references to Appendices
Ribemont	4/5/16		500 mills grenade carriers received from Corps.	
—	5/5/16		Routine work	
—	6/5/16		800 steel helmets received, issued proportionately to all troops who are exposed positions & been issued — attempting to receive from Corps	
—	7/5/16		500 mills grenade carriers received from Contract. 35 packets	
—	8/5/16		Shell receivers after conversion	
—	9/5/16		Routine work. Inferences Corps re Mr Tate Jr Henry Trench huts Nissen. At present they are being supplied from Bath Stone from the provisional leads last allow for Hudson & Elphs patterns	
—	10/5/16		McArthur work	
—	11/5/16		Further 1400 Steel Helmets received from Corps.	

Army Form C. 2118

WAR DIARY
or
INTELLIGENCE SUMMARY
(Erase heading not required.)

Instructions regarding War Diaries and Intelligence Summaries are contained in F. S. Regs., Part II. and the Staff Manual respectively. Title Pages will be prepared in manuscript.

Place	Date	Hour	Summary of Events and Information	Remarks and references to Appendices
Rivennes	12/5/16		Question of extracting of Spelr Pun from huts Bindes. Field how Plein consulered necessary. Application for Bivvouac huts to Corps.	
"	13/	"	Colouring other than Clitch is found necessary to conceal tents &c. It is understood that a suitable camouflage mixture is in course of preparation at Base.	
"	14/	"	Trévun Aubin	
"	15/	"	have fresh arrangement to ensure a supper turnover of Pill Snipers held in Divisional Reserve.	
"	16/	"	Collected 20 handcarts for heavy Trench Mortar Batteries as heavy howitz Droupes. General	
"	17/	"	Intent to Rear for Pitt G. Heewitt for R.A. (clerk) notices replacing made	
"	18/	"	her Typing magazine for Lewis Gun which most expecting. Forwarded agent	
"	19/	"	to XV Corps in Every torday.	
"	20/	"	Return Alin	
"	21/	"		

1875 Wt: W593/826 1,000,000 4/15 J.B.C. & A. A.D.S.S./Forms/C. 2118.

Army Form C. 2118

WAR DIARY
or
INTELLIGENCE SUMMARY
(Erase heading not required.)

Instructions regarding War Diaries and Intelligence Summaries are contained in F. S. Regs., Part II. and the Staff Manual respectively. Title Pages will be prepared in manuscript.

Place	Date	Hour	Summary of Events and Information	Remarks and references to Appendices
Riencourt	22/5/16		Intervention in Montauban of XV Corps Armouring repairs to various Lorries	
"	23/		R.E. instruments etc. Distinguishing Badges for various units in Div. Consolidating demands for	
"	24/		Great Puncture ratify duties.	
"	25/		Return of Prisoners (2 men) processing Palgaebride & reports of Bonnets of transfer coming in.	
"	26/		Arabic work	
"	27/		Application for supply of Electric Signalling lamps refused by Corps.	
"	28/		Replies to letters enquiring into reason between A.O.D. & Salvage Co.	
"	29/		Returned 100 pieces of Harness with own ships to Divisn to Vipelend Pennetiers.	
"	30/		letter received from Army stating that in future H.M. mud seen out The equipment in Shed they annihilate began having it replaced.	
"	31/		4 Sets of Splinter Guns delivered (3 from Bt Div.) + 1 from 87 Corps).	

R Martin. Capt.
DADOS 21. DIV.

Army Form C. 2118

WAR DIARY
or
INTELLIGENCE SUMMARY
(Erase heading not required.)

DADOS 21 DV
Vol 9

Place	Date	Hour	Summary of Events and Information	Remarks and references to Appendices
Abbeville	1/6/16		Purchase & Issue of material for Chatty [?] fishing Baskets.	
	2/-		Proposed 75 m Flea [?] of Plans for extracting splinters of Mills Bombs rejected as being to expensive. A deep dugout in the grounds of Rest hotel inspected.	
	3/-		Several days of firm wet district	
	4/-		Hun Lewis Gun magazines very defective in the last issue. Many sprung found to be Russian. Report rendered to XIV Corps Ordinance.	
	5/-		Claim. Statement for Trench howitzer Batteries and defficiency [?] for heavy Ammunition. A heavier gun to be being retained for R.E. Park. Plans indefinite.	
	6/-		Martin Cartier [?]	
	7/-		Arrangements made for XIV Corps workshops to find extra fittings in Pitt. Cert.	
	8/-		Martin Mulin [?]	
	9/-		Ten thousand rounds of small arm Ammunition (Pistol) being returned to E Sun [?] as too heavy been issued for them since the E.O.O. been purchased as no call has ever been made for them. Old Pitt. Pattern an expensive used for this purpose.	

Army Form C. 2118

Instructions regarding War Diaries and Intelligence
Summaries are contained in F. S. Regs., Part II.
and the Staff Manual respectively. Title Pages
will be prepared in manuscript.

WAR DIARY
or
INTELLIGENCE SUMMARY
(Erase heading not required.)

Place	Date	Hour	Summary of Events and Information	Remarks and references to Appendices
Riennes	22/5/16		Interviews with Interpreters of XV Corps Armies reports to various Stores, P.T. instruments etc.	
"	23/	-	Distinguishing Badges for various units in Div. Consolidating demands for Great Puncture Rehef duties.	
"	24/	-	Return of Armourers (2- per man) pieces Rifle cartridges + reports of Boards	
"	25/	-	of Survey Comm in Ambler work.	
"	26/	-	Application for supply of electric signalling lamps referred to Corps.	
"	27/	-	Replies to Corps enquiry into reserve between F.O.D. + Salvage Coy.	
"	28/	-	Salvaged 100 pieces of harness with coin clips to serve as Keyless Pincers.	
"	29/	-	Letter received from Army stating that in draft Murrel serves out The Equipment in Short	
"	30/	-	they arrived but have begun having it replaced. (3 from R. Div.) + 1 from 87 Corps).	
"	31/	-	4 Rear Spring Springs received	

J. R. Martin, Capt.
D.A.D.O.S. 21. DIV.

Army Form C. 2118

DADOS 21 3rd
VOL 9

WAR DIARY
or
INTELLIGENCE SUMMARY
(Erase heading not required.)

Instructions regarding War Diaries and Intelligence Summaries are contained in F. S. Regs., Part II. and the Staff Manual respectively. Title Pages will be prepared in manuscript.

Place	Date	Hour	Summary of Events and Information	Remarks and references to Appendices
Abbeville	1/6/16		Purchase & payment of material for distribution ordered.	
	2/-		Proposed to the Flash Infield Plans full extraction of Mills Bomb rejected as being to a repair. A deep dug-out being constructed for storing these in Amiens.	
	3/-		General Gunning district	
	4/-		New Lewis Gun Magazines very defective in the new pain, heavy grease found to be rotten before use. Reports rendered to XII Corps reference this.	
	5/-		Plans & statements for Trench Mortar Batteries and details supplied for R. E. Parc. War reserve	
	6/-		Arrangements made for XIII Corps workshops to find extra fittings in SAA.	
	7/-		Confr.	
	8/-		Muslim duties.	
	9/-		The harmful reserve of Steel Pots. Helmets (Pattern) being returned to Sun as no call has ever been made for them since the E.C.O. was published. Bed Pitt. Pattern on approval used for this purpose.	

Army Form C. 2118

WAR DIARY
or
INTELLIGENCE SUMMARY
(Erase heading not required.)

Place	Date	Hour	Summary of Events and Information	Remarks and references to Appendices
Vieuxmont	10/6/16		Lines Section of Special Coy R.E. under Monte Breck carries out of Gun Groups to appeals of light helmets.	
	11/		Instruction duties.	
	12/		Large demands for blades of all kinds; wind appears to be insufficient however.	
	13/		hi.	
	14/		hi. Experimental Section (100 per batty Coil) of Viglem Ridges i', 3' Bg Meen of mining Em.	
	15/		Ground Section from Div. Helios to Renewal Boo mon Centreto.	
	16/		Recently has instructor for Div Gloves sleep inf.	
	17/		hi.	
	18/		hi.	
	19/		Visited Div. Glenn & formed them his not in possession of new hot Pen.	
	20/		Table due to the re - organisation of Artillery.	

Army Form C. 2118

WAR DIARY
or
INTELLIGENCE SUMMARY
(Erase heading not required.)

Instructions regarding War Diaries and Intelligence Summaries are contained in F. S. Regs., Part II. and the Staff Manual respectively. Title Pages will be prepared in manuscript.

Place	Date	Hour	Summary of Events and Information	Remarks and references to Appendices
Ploegsteert	21/-	—	Large demands by units for stores in excess of establishment. Gowns keeping Cutters hire. Vigilant Patrols kept to have been kept by Brec picheras.	
"	22/-	—	607 Canvas Water Bags received from 4th Army to-day.	
"	23/-	—	75 "ddrs" rec'd Reaction for Back lights No 7.	
"	24/-	—	Practice duties.	
"	25/-	—	Division 7.5" + Carriage completed cleaned. Standard 26 Mylar 75 Heavy shot for Trench Mortars (T.M.).	
"	26/-	—	Workshops cleaned for conversion for Rifle mechanism.	
"	27/-	—	(Rifles) On 18 pdr. battery action int. damaged at Ypres Cam. Du 2" Trench mortar completely destroyed.	
"	28/-	—	Du 2" Trench mortar completely destroyed by shell fire.	
"	29/-	—	act 6. Two 3" Stokes Guns and one 18 pdr. (running out of spring) out of action. Two Lewis Guns and	
"	30/-	—		

T. A. Pravini Capt.
DADOS. 21. Div. Steadier.
B. E. F.

21/ Army Form C. 2118
July
SADS

WAR DIARY
or
INTELLIGENCE SUMMARY
(Erase heading not required.)

Vol 10

Place	Date	Hour	Summary of Events and Information	Remarks and references to Appendices
Ribemont	1/7/16		In charge of burial site for Suffers: Small reserve held by me for emergencies.	
"	2 & 3rd		Continuation of above.	
"	4/-		Lt Bonner ?	
Mailly-Maillet	5/-		Large quantities of stores received from here urgently required to be quite insufficient to make Battalion being in action. Confer the four buried here to be made to clear the dump. Three parties. Three monkeys had to carry Depo horses.	
"	6/-		A few units are able to attend dumps to draw stores only as a further hour return their transport waggons to every extra stores drawn.	
"	7/-			
"	8/-		hour to Carieux.	
Carieux	9/-		Several units able to attend dumps to draw stores. Guidance of Neuhaus	
"	10/-		renders carrying Lorry punctuals at they clearing thin and taking from 10	
"	11/-		a few outlying units.	
"	12/-		Have been to XV Corps area w/r dumps & movement of ASC.	

WAR DIARY
or
INTELLIGENCE SUMMARY
(Erase heading not required.)

Army Form C. 2118

Place	Date	Hour	Summary of Events and Information	Remarks and references to Appendices
Mericourt	13/7/16		The 110th tgy Bde Shoe Coln & the Div. has 63½% full equipt & far is clothing was concerned Gen. Thu. is of in a period ch. equips the Bde. The Bde. is at the 110 th & went to relieve fire. Sevi Gun detachments in large proportion were being trained for gun fighting and by Train in what were unable to bring them are the general report on their elements is that they are unable for the purpose infantry and are more an extra burden than any assistance. R. to 21mm Divin convoyed.	
"	14.15.16 & 17 & 18/-		G. Bury to several changes for distribution. to Dist. Admin. C.R.E. convoy to that Batterfui. have been to Carvillers (3 miles distant). Took train lorry Convoy (Shois is improvement & injurid 21 mm. & have improvement made at turners. to bring the Pdr to Ecouloirs (ments) back & had Food in service this matter here is important.	
"	19/- 20/-		have To E Cavary VII Corps III Army men (9¾ km G. Cany.)	

Army Form C. 2118

WAR DIARY
or
INTELLIGENCE SUMMARY
(Erase heading not required.)

Place	Date	Hour	Summary of Events and Information	Remarks and references to Appendices
St Cloud	2/7/16		Party collecting his Torpy Evans & stones from Carriere and Newport. In extra Corps acquired a appreciation.	
		22 to 30.7.	Very occupied with lines Chin ammunition. Over thousand lets gear from the had any immediate demands. 117th Division is strong over 11,000 and Reinforcements have been kept by me at moment to replace them being taken over by	
		17.15 pm		
Divisions	30/7/16 31/-		From 1st Division to dump occupied by them 11.15 am. No shells for America received from them.	

Approved Capt. 2.10 pm
Capt & 31/7/16

Appen P 1916 Missing

✓ WHEN MARKING UP DOCUMENTS FOR COPYING PLEASE TICK THE APPROPRIATE BOX ON THE OPPOSITE SIDE OF THIS MARKER. THIS INFORMATION IS ESSENTIAL TO ALLOW US TO PROVIDE YOU WITH THE COPIES YOU REQUIRE INFORMATION SHEETS ARE AVAILABLE FROM THE RECORD COPYING COUNTER SHOULD YOU NEED FURTHER ASSISTANCE. ***

Army Form C. 2118

WAR DIARY
or
INTELLIGENCE SUMMARY
(Erase heading not required.)

Instructions regarding War Diaries and Intelligence Summaries are contained in F. S. Regs., Part II. and the Staff Manual respectively. Title Pages will be prepared in manuscript.

Place	Date	Hour	Summary of Events and Information	Remarks and references to Appendices
DUISANS	1/9/16 to 4/9/16		Position austere. Steps being [taken] re movement The manoeuvre in view of forthcoming move.	
LE CAUROY	5/9/16 to 12/9/16		Move to Le Cauroy. Four Lorries deputed to transport stores & personnel less Smoke Helmets. On our far all ranks were had opportunity of being in billets & making up arrears of sleep. Consumate efforts made to renew his clothing (a clean) to each airty sentry. Special arrangement made to renew his clothing & furniture to every man began marching ones to his own & to collect cloths & sentry to the Ras was March on two has own (47 Army) arranged with R.T.O. at Cauroy to being conveyed by Rail. As being convinced that just as an instruction enough before Helmets could have been re-introduced also, been charged en route to Further Helmets could (for Div. fit for long service. The very useful precaution any changes of weather & chances of storm to every emergency. Arrange that head to it held up 5000. our emergency Army has been received.	
RISEMONT	14/9/16		Establishing a temporary dump.	
CARCHILLOT FARM.	15/9/16		Moved to the Station in accordance the storm of recent transport lines & rail head.	

1875 Wt. W593/826 1,000,000 4/15 J.B.C. & A. A.D.S.S./Forms/C. 2118.

Place	Date	Hour	Summary of Events and Information	Remarks and references to Appendices
CARCHILOT FARM	16/9/16		Visited various Dumps collecting Stres Helmets. Dis. handed in this morning two Thorny[?] shed. Buried for some work, had been in for some weeks. Hypoians[?] were returned to equip the Infantry + Artillery. Pay duty visits to Infantry + Artillery H.Q. Captain arranged the stores for unit's, store Transport Linis are beyond the arranges of Corris on forwarded to travel to various dumps through the night when stores possible. When the trains are trucking, storms are hasted up.	
	to		Begins stone possible. Div Column ups down to Infantry to B Echelon. Div Column All R.F.A. Horses are accepted + Transport by + decides R.F.A. tho. in possession in jutting vehicles as demand it. Difficulty is in communication, but many cases unit are not supply to continue through and to visit unit in charge of the Cars to relings Sup. to monochat get l refrigeration any damaged vehicle + others in effect a repair enough to hand Six GS Wagon B'omb into other to must anticipate augmentation of replacement. The transport of clothing returned from an has been to rest further raking this clothing stock with for use trange. Dis. was comple full of water. Mr. was further when seen carnin running a project invnailsthe of newcar when clean. Arrangements being male for further blackets + return of daily clothing.	
	30/9/16			T. Afrroi. Capt. D.A.D.O.S. 2, O.M. 30/9/16.

VOL 13

Army Form C. 2118

WAR DIARY
or
INTELLIGENCE SUMMARY
(Erase heading not required.)

Place	Date	Hour	Summary of Events and Information	Remarks and references to Appendices
ONGICHOT FARM.	1 & 2 10/6		As Division is to leave the Somme front in the 3rd arrangements are made with D.T.O. at Albert in connection with the delivery to his destination Boro dell' Conquete of J.B.G. Clothing delivered to Corps Dysentery Hospital at Pucheraux changes in convoys of action. Leave for II Corps area. A.D.M.S. & Head-Quarters.	
"	3/-		As we are to stay to lend a hand & finish has arranged to remove stores from Vignacourt (X Corps) to 1st Corps Railhead.	
"	4/- 5/- 6/-		Leave for 1st Corps hours etc. known.	
"	7/- A.S.C to 12th		Received elements for 1 fun two Blankets, as it is found the 1st Corps appear that a Thirst in Johnson through the transfer works & in 25th of strength as is The 4th Army.	
Jennerer	13/-		Move to Labourse & take over dumps from 87 D.U.	

WAR DIARY
or
INTELLIGENCE SUMMARY
(Erase heading not required.)

Army Form C. 2118

Place	Date	Hour	Summary of Events and Information	Remarks and references to Appendices
Lahore	14/7/16	10	Prepare demands for Water Bottles. Thrown 4000 pairs of Gum Boots. Thigh Ind. 3250 ors, & similar number find P.T. Bts.	
	18/7/16		Visit Corps & Army Ordnance Workshops and an interest in the obtaining of Rear stores in the Army.	
"	19/7/16		Thistle Helmets received from I Jar all ranks 10 5000. Complete returned to hand of obtaining a demand warring stock skin	
"	24/7/16		Asked ordnance 1st Augustus Summons of manner. Arrival of 533 thousand with ammunition Lt. Arthur Ministry stores of Telearplatier VDQ 69 Bde. Stone ready No 1 Division Coy.	
"	29/7/16		Return duties.	
	26/ -		All Gunns of Div Rats from Tkrugh Shaugh. Return of Gunnis P.O. kinder Over to 1 Otk. Charge Letter to Divisional Ajgn in Chief orders v Ammunition in allotment is at forward march in this Corps.	

Army Form C. 2118

WAR DIARY
or
INTELLIGENCE SUMMARY
(Erase heading not required.)

Instructions regarding War Diaries and Intelligence Summaries are contained in F.S. Regs., Part II. and the Staff Manual respectively. Title Pages will be prepared in manuscript.

Place	Date	Hour	Summary of Events and Information	Remarks and references to Appendices
Lahore	27/10/16 to 3/11/16		Stores Rugs &c received to form. Also six Henco Cliff's Machine ones to town. 1 fan been Kilwicks has been received and is fitted. Two lamps Hurricane allotted to Division to light the several units in the Division are equipped with 2 Field Kitchen + 1 G.S. Wagon instead of 4 Kitchens. Report of G.S. Wagon for Kitchen passed to Bank. The Formation of Divisional Train to 2 instead of 4 Coarse Squad orderly is clearly outlined. Regiments will use it enemy coming up from town, The Kitchens to be furnished after 7 p.m.	

1/11/16

Algernon Cpt.
ADOW 25 DW

WAR DIARY
or
INTELLIGENCE SUMMARY
(Erase heading not required.)

Army Form C. 2118

DADOS
21 Div
/14

Place	Date	Hour	Summary of Events and Information	Remarks and references to Appendices
LABOURSE	1+2/11/16		From Aughnacloy arrived at Bazincourt. Recd. Instrn. for return of horse from transp. etc. → Capt/R.L. Quarrie proceeded on leave to England.	
LABOURSE	3/11/16	pm	Visited Light workshops Bethune thereat over 72 Running out spring? who gave army Sm. inside workshops. knew abt 30 different Enfield Rifle mechanisms for 2" T.M. Informant Foreman of Thickness there were 7 to make this out of action for the want of Enfield Rifle supply promised for 4-11-16. Journey Reformed by heavy Lorry.	
—	4/16	—	140 bombs. Metal Ribbon (Militar head) 10 for mission Cross — 4/11/16 delivered at DHS HQ. for Prevention ⅃-Corps Commander on 5/11/16 Cronin's Circuits) One 2" T Mortar Rgt No 407 received from X21 Thirlwall for a Temple Airness K1 fitted unable to found it to the, while workshops as the 2 lorries were employed till 6.30 pm no car was available. 2" T.M. No 407 and Enfield Rifle for 3 Ton Lorry. Le Enforcer Rifle mechanisms intended for to complete to code — 20 required.	
—	5/11/16	—		
—	6/16	—	26 Lewis guns received, to complete units to 10 per Bn . . . 6 Cannied for stores Ammunition received from RE workshops, 2 waiters to enot Rhe for Fril. Visited Corp No 21 Ost. Workshops also 1st Army ly Shops.	

Army Form C. 2118

WAR DIARY
or
INTELLIGENCE SUMMARY
(Erase heading not required.)

Instructions regarding War Diaries and Intelligence Summaries are contained in F.S. Regs., Part II. and the Staff Manual respectively. Title Pages will be prepared in manuscript.

Place	Date	Hour	Summary of Events and Information	Remarks and references to Appendices
LABOURSE	7/11/16	—	Routine work.	
"	8/11/16	—	Visited No 1 Ord. Shops re Plugs for 2" T.M. adapters. Reviews from No 1 Ord. Workshops Tm. 2" No 247 after alteration to receive Temple silencer. 2" T.M. Regd No 226 reservoir damaged — unable to send to workshops as no Transport now available.	
"	9/11/16	—	2" Tm. No 326 sent to Mob. mobile workshop for Lorry. Routine work.	
"	10/11/16	—	Visited No 1 Ord: workshop, also First Army Gr. mobile workshop. Arranged to draw 1 - 2" T.m. after repair 50 flat wires + 1 floorboard for bty Hqrs. on 12-11-16. 75 Lanterns F.D. reissued to each of 62 & 64 Bdes from those received for use in +10145 Bdes under orders of D.A.D.O.S. M.A. From those received for use in Billets owing to the Shortage of Candles + the necessarie for lights in dugouts.	
"	12/11/16	—	Routine work.	
"	13/11/16	11 AM	Office & dumps visited by DDOS First Army + ADOS I Corps	

WAR DIARY
or
INTELLIGENCE SUMMARY
(Erase heading not required.)

Army Form C. 2118

Place	Date	Hour	Summary of Events and Information	Remarks and references to Appendices
LABOURSE	14/6	10.30	Difficulty experienced in obtaining 2,000 Francs to purchase stone from Cashier I Corps who would not accept the written permission of Capt Quennie, the largest holder, to his Conf. foreman XV A.O.C. during Capt Quennies temporary absence on leave. Corps Routine Order No 7 dated 6th Nov 1916 was complied with. The amount was paid after about 2 hours waiting time. The Cashier evidently was not acquainted with para 290 Kings Regt & para 625 R.A.O.C. Part. I 1912.	
		pm	Capt Rennie returned off leave and resumed duty as D.A.D.O.S. 21st.	M Brennen Capt

WAR DIARY
or
INTELLIGENCE SUMMARY
(Erase heading not required.)

Army Form C. 2118

Place	Date	Hour	Summary of Events and Information	Remarks and references to Appendices
LABOURSE	15/11/16		Four Army Bearers to Transfer Officers ordered to units & Carlyerte ordered for this work Indian Cavalry Corps.	
	16 to 24/11/16		Rest of duties. Capt. G.S. Spindler Canadian Ordnance, reported here on the 17th.	
	20/11 to 25/11/16		Routine to Clair Hammer under Army Instructions. Arranged programme with 10th Lys W Sup. Return re Divisional Establishment.	
	26 to 30/11/16		In demands for Stores Books. In trues are now improved. Men's kits have been returned to Base.	
	3/11/16		Percentage return of men clothing & equipment much improved. Routine duties.	

5/12/16

R. [signature]
Major
RAMC
2i/c

—

D.A.D.O.S Army Form C. 2118
21st Division
Vol 15

WAR DIARY
or
INTELLIGENCE SUMMARY
(Erase heading not required.)

Place	Date	Hour	Summary of Events and Information	Remarks and references to Appendices
Lahorre	1/12/16 to 15/12/16		Routine work. First Circuit. Inspected Ammunition Dumps. Spent three days in Divisional Ammn Dump. Forwarded through D Corps recommendation that Lewis drummers be given use of W.D. Gun. Carried in arm experiment with 2" trench mortar Rifle mechanism. Great trouble getting supply of cups. Then an improvement nig w/ be effected by adoption of 4 LOG = cups then the average weight of rifle mechanism is 15 to 12 hours the average weight of rifle mechanism is approximately sixteen.	
Lahorre	11/12/16 to 28/12/16		Demand transmitted to Base to Corps to secure of 2000 jackets. Trousers & Putties. Arrears of 123 Trousers & Putties is steadily being reduced by Base in their general stores. Bando Party returned to Base not replaced by units under 2 per man can be permitted to allow for washing. Complaints on the Supply Shirts m men of superior instead of no boots not upheld by Divisional Headquarters.	

WAR DIARY
or
INTELLIGENCE SUMMARY
(Erase heading not required.)

Army Form C. 2118

Place	Date	Hour	Summary of Events and Information	Remarks and references to Appendices
Jerusalem	28/3/16		Leave Jerusalem for rail head. Only Two lorries available + as the rail dump has not been repaired, an Ordnance Depot began here to carry all classes.	
			Sent to Conveyance to Jerusalem for one day delivery of stores from Base.	
Jerusalem	29/3/16 to 3/4/16		Take over new depot in Jerusalem was Salvage Coy. Reported to Major I. Cooper then in personal command of Jerusalem in Inacceviable clothing. Survey of Bicycles & Leave from Armoured Stys & Distr. Coll. to Light Ordnance Mobile Workshop proceed on that work only.	

Ephraim Cyr.
N.O.M.
ZION

WAR DIARY
or
INTELLIGENCE SUMMARY
(Erase heading not required.)

Army Form C. 2118

D.A.D.O.S 21st Division

Vol 16

Place	Date	Hour	Summary of Events and Information	Remarks and references to Appendices
Lahoussoye	1/1/17		Arrange programme for overhaul of all Travelling Kitchens & Limbers Waterhyds. This is being carried out on the same lines as Water Carts 30% of their hair already passed through workshops. Iron Shields to be replaced & limbers G.S. Wagons. Experiments & experimentation put in hand pending of Iron Wagons for carriage of limber in Refit Time	
			Many Complaints received from units concerning the scarcity of F.S.B.nts. The lastest appears to be by more by even greater to previous refuse. Owing to Change of Programme organising men & Ordnance stores from Boots & to men fit [Programme] standard. being not in just the number of Shaft horses demanded has kept very heavy	
			(X of Leather ½ Rounds)	
	15/1/17		Issue Puncture of 120 Sam Cookers per Brigade (40 per Brigade)	

WAR DIARY
or
INTELLIGENCE SUMMARY
(Erase heading not required.)

Army Form C. 2118

Place	Date	Hour	Summary of Events and Information	Remarks and references to Appendices
Lahore	16/1/17		Routine duties.	
	28/1/17		Guns received & equipment arriving from Bari & S.D. Centring store movements. Rtn. was reported to A/QMG. I Corps & Sample of clothing returned as 'U' returned for material. Bangy to notify O.i/c. Hosps. that 95% of clothing returned as 'U' is merely dirty & could be made serviceable by immediate & constant P.R.O. particulars to this effect.	
	28/1/17		Orders for 250 Yellow & Black Flags for Signals. Between Lahore & Jullundur 1 R.T. Officers to hand over to Bairn. Stores dump put to East — from 30 miles about. Old Receiver Sections available & units (trans.) to hold down orders not being able to collect stores from being collected can pay for them on writing to this function; man se gun left work can refer wit J surplus receipts from Stores received from Sialkot & Rulhur Stores due to reorganisation. Stryam receipts returned.	
	3/1/17		Further dump & movement. Sent Rt. to Commandant to collect more useful Card.	
Rawalpindi Stn			Report driving from Saw:	

McGervin Capt.
DADS
Z.P.W.

WAR DIARY
or
INTELLIGENCE SUMMARY
Army Form C. 2118

DADOS
21st Div
Vol 17

Place	Date	Hour	Summary of Events and Information	Remarks and references to Appendices
HOUCHOUT	1/2/17		Local formation of feelers. Rebel Flags for Keeps also of Pour Colmun. handcar from DCups to VIII Corps area with pigeoment by heats advanced Lewis Gun standards. 2"Trench mortar minous & Lewis in Charge of Bowe site not suggest replacements. Climaters not of available but also in mund. Chips advised d'astre to provide indents in Charge as temporary meanin pending arrival of Klinomiters. P.O. Sprints from Left Div DAMP I Army. Belled muzzion of Vippers.	
BETHUNE	9/2/17		(Return to I Corps area. Represention to I Corps in record of Regd 15 Cars. Car been in than to provide Immunis Car. Tel heavy unconnumed Immunis had to be payment by 5th Cavic not Covers of 2, 3 CoM mtg.	

WAR DIARY
or
INTELLIGENCE SUMMARY
(Erase heading not required.)

Army Form C. 2118

Place	Date	Hour	Summary of Events and Information	Remarks and references to Appendices
Bethune	16/2/17		Arrange with A.D.V.S. to visit our dumps tomorrow.	
Lecouse	17/2/17		Ten own 6ⁿᵈ Div. dumps. On first two days in them 21 Py. G. treatment for 2ⁿᵈ Trench horses as received unsound. Great difficulty experienced in obtaining replacements. 2 Infantry Brigades of 4th Div. to nearby of J.D. Cavalry Brigade. The men had approved been made up to new basis in going Brigades. Clothing orderless rather ready for return to Base. Trenches & observed this to be observed not allowed. Their inspection number is necessary for Rations.	
	21/2/17		Transport. With recluse less than a week observed. Satisfactorily. Visit Lorry Col. 53² of Lancashire Corps in reference 2ⁿᵈ Trench transport. Men well informed by R. Base as Reinforcements had been in replacement. As T. Telemeters an S/Lieut available at Post T.M. Co. authorized. As T. Telemeters are S/Lieut not available at Post T.M. Co. in Company, using 50%. W/O obtaining from stores. 4.D.V. informed & is Corespond. D.O.V. asked to see Frenchman Chief farriery races of Claremont Etc.	

WAR DIARY
or
INTELLIGENCE SUMMARY
(Erase heading not required.)

Army Form C. 2118

Place	Date	Hour	Summary of Events and Information	Remarks and references to Appendices
Lahore	24/3/17		Owing to condition of Trenches Conveyance in the Rear is to Ensure necessary for Infantry to take Change of Posts daily. There is improved from Pekat 21 due to 6800 Divisional reserve. Eight camels & 10000 without. Demand on R.O.S.T. for 11 timbered G.S. Wagons for carriage of leave from (Campbelpore Tunnel). No Boys have arrived from Khan for Town inside. T.O Army Authorize as previously. R.S. hadin Indian.	
"	28/3/17			

W. Grasin Cap.
A.D.M.S. 21st Dn
2/3/17.

WAR DIARY
INTELLIGENCE SUMMARY

D.A.D.O.S. 21st Division

Vol 18

Place	Date	Hour	Summary of Events and Information	Remarks and references to Appendices
LA BOURSE	1/3/17		Arrange through AOMS I Corps to hand over all "RAID" stores assembled during French wagon over to 6th Div. & 24th Div. respectively.	
"	2/3/17		Drove to Etrus[?] in support of letter written arrangement made to meet their issue to RAMC AOC &c as personnel + mar to Extra Carriage West Road to been issued convenient meaning of this time of the year. Experimental separation on S.E. Sideboard Wagon for carrying of Rabbit Fish in carrying Instruments and lid convenient to hypo. Stop lid. Seal also entry to be sent of a Divisional Superintendent Nargh. Const. Arm. Baijon Cart to 6th Div. (Supt. RFA (Right Sect. RE.) in new of superseding suspension of this Div. for 4th Army. Arrange to hand a N.O.	
"	3/3/17		to hdd hor Ethical to carry m in Engineers with this Div.	
"	4/3/17		Interviewing G.O.C. Div. Re RFA in provision of 105 for Battery demonstration. Advise this number be considered to be reserve if one of our driven from rough country and in ablies.	

Army Form C. 2118.

WAR DIARY
or
INTELLIGENCE SUMMARY.
(Erase heading not required.)

Place	Date	Hour	Summary of Events and Information	Remarks and references to Appendices
LABOURSE	5/3/17		Routine duties.	
	6/3/17		On recpt of requisition Large quantities of Perambulators for carriage of Ammunition issued to Divs. That the requisition of 1/26 per Divl. seemed [?] low in the circumstances with the invention of allowance.	
	7/3/17		On ascertaining that a quantity of mature cloths [?] allotted to Infantry for a charge in connection of Trenches was requested I had the General's sanction to his Dirt Quarter Supply for the cloths & rendered to Infant that unit on leaving the Area use agt removal of blankets & came directly to III Army. This was protested to AQN+I Army.	
	9/3/17		G/Hq Extra Emergency Ration of Distinguished from Preserved checking horses allowance until D+T Quartermaster made on each unit above of future supply.	
	15/3/17		Proceed to III Army have to 15/3/17 to ascertain Dumps of broken Arrangements completed for clearing reached by hour transport when instructions can isd to OC's batteries. Lt. Col. Bryerman G.E. Div. reviews. Repair to + OM III Corps re apply for opin of Corps Traction Engine.	

Army Form C. 2118.

WAR DIARY
or
INTELLIGENCE SUMMARY.
(Erase heading not required.)

Instructions regarding War Diaries and Intelligence Summaries are contained in F.S. Regs., Part II. and the Staff Manual respectively. Title pages will be prepared in manuscript.

Place	Date	Hour	Summary of Events and Information	Remarks and references to Appendices
LUCHEUX	16/3/17	—	Capt: R.W. Mattie, D.A.D.S.T. proceeded on leave.	
		12.50 pm	A.D.S.T. VII Corps. (Lt-Col: Attwerman) visited office. Routine work	
	17/3/17	—	Units report on tow state of trucks which left the march to VII Corps Area. 18 pairs repaired in our shop. Whilst the new wooden showtage in supply of leather. — Expert supply of boots received from Anne at 4.30 p.m. + issue made to 3 Button Batts B.E.F. — Remainder of units dealt with on 18th	
		2 p.m.	Proceeded to Domino to remove canvas packsaddlery	
		M.N.	Received a report to A.D.S.T. VII Corps re the "overlap", in demanding small stores on the same day + sometimes on the day before. Similar letters arrive.	
			One lorry from tr. 13th N.F. + one 3" A.T.F. Ko. for both T.M. Bty. received from Brent.	
	18/3/17	9 p.m.	Sent two lorries to O.O. Army Troops N°2 to remove Tentage to S.12.B.	
			14 N.F. (Pioneers) rejoined the Division from 2 weeks. Received 24 hours. Received	
			Army Corps: to complete Dept's Bns (less Pioneers) to 1000 each. Army.	
			3/2 Reb packsaddlery. Army 'Phones air. 1 Pr. that R.S.D.	
			BOUQUEMAISON has commenced. Army 'Phones air. 1 Pr. that R.S.D. BOUQUEMAISON has commenced. A.D.S.T. Army 'Phones tht 4 trucks at Railhead have been ordered.	
			The 4 M.T. lorries were utilised, 2 to bring underclothing from BETHUNE and two to remove tents to static dump. Railhead was closed to 4-15 p.m. by Notre (A13) which reported late.	

Army Form C. 2118.

WAR DIARY
or
INTELLIGENCE SUMMARY.
(Erase heading not required.)

Instructions regarding War Diaries and Intelligence Summaries are contained in F. S. Regs., Part II. and the Staff Manual respectively. Title pages will be prepared in manuscript.

Place	Date	Hour	Summary of Events and Information	Remarks and references to Appendices
LUCHEUX	19/3/17		37th Divisional Artillery moves to Divn: from VIth Divn: also 37th T.M. Bty. with No 1 Coy 37th D. Francis. Routine work	
	20/3/17		Lts N: Notified that OC 2/1 8 per No 767 of A.B. 96 7th Bde had been condemned by EOM & was gun remainer in Indent (wire) & y.7.R.	
		9.15AM	Proceeded to AMIENS to collect 40 canvas packsaddle bags for Amm'n: ammn' & Ration Carriers for Infantry. Had to proceed by lorry - Journey Corr- police by 6.10 pm. Routine work.	
	21/3/17		One AO/ZQMy ordered to report to CRE by 9 A.M. and one officer to proceed to ANVIN to collect R.A. stores left behind during the last march. 8 M.T. lorry drivers taken on Ration strength owing to distance from HQ. No 8 Supply Col: Good amounts of stores received from Base also lentils and jewlery. Routine work	
	22/3/17		Routine work.	
	23/3/17	10.45am	Camp visited by AOP Third Army, who enquired as to the quantity of gas, grease & smokeletts available in the event of a forward movement.	
		11 Am	Office stamp visited by A.D.V.S. VIIth Corps. Records, books outstanding	

WAR DIARY or INTELLIGENCE SUMMARY

Army Form C. 2118.

3

Place	Date	Hour	Summary of Events and Information	Remarks and references to Appendices
LUCHEUX	28/3/17		Intends to go into Batt Bdes: inspected. Present system of reading Mail items viewed, to be reviewed, so as to bring into line with other divns.	
		8 AM	One MgA lorry reported as having engine trouble could not proceed to Div at GOUY. Hired M.T. Supply Col. to send assistance. Lorry was at GRAND-RULLECOURT. Second lorry reported damaged + sent to Supply Col.	
	26/3/17	9 AM	2 ATD lorries sent to St MICHEL, 2 miles E of St POL to remove 21st TDM Bde. + 95th Bde: HQ. to LUCHEUX.	
		11 AM	RQD BOUQUEMAISON wired that Railhead administration closed. One lorry to replace a lorry reported arrived at Dumps at 12.15 P.M. + was requested to Railhead, which was cleared by 4 P.M.	
	25/3/17		Routine work. 95th Bde RQM No. 2 Sec. 21st DHC rejoined distr from Batt D. 11 to Labour Coy: Rm. Infantry + 7th Infantry Labour Coy: joined distr from 30th Division.	
	26/3/17		37th Fd Artillery M.O.T Coy, 37 Armis + 1/2 12 HR Labour Dr. moved to 14 Stn. Routine work.	

Army Form C. 2118.

WAR DIARY
or
INTELLIGENCE SUMMARY.
(Erase heading not required.)

Instructions regarding War Diaries and Intelligence Summaries are contained in F. S. Regs., Part II. and the Staff Manual respectively. Title pages will be prepared in manuscript.

Place	Date	Hour	Summary of Events and Information	Remarks and references to Appendices
LUCHEUX	27/3/17		Received notice that requirements would be supplied from Southern Base - list of units administered, provided to COs where possible. Capt. R.L.D. Morrie returned off leave & resumed duty as adjutant.	
"	28/3/17		2 W.O.s Cert. admin. in department to Sanity Pari. Musician Civil PS. Cannd. D.R.O. To be published warning inhabitants of 15 minutes Telescopic Explosion. Previous for to explain this item to Men by armourer.	
LaCAUCHIE	29/3/17		Adjutant given fol procedure of to Canada where man Army Group to Refugee to explain effected. 370 Bell Tunic + khaki supplies to requirements of 5th Don. Jam. One list to issued to 76 Chin Army Troops Consul. Dump Dem Kmitz.	
"	30/3/17		New Scheme for Posting to Incheux area hours to 5th D. Don Vast XXX III Corps + Chinese arranging for supply of Drammer Boys during an advance.	
"	31/3/17		Drummer Boys between Trenches & tren in Communistic Dumps. R.E. & Pai Ahalis to utilize for extreme duties. Instead reported to AOH III Corps in that ability in that moving military during evolution operas. Afghanis Capt. 21 OU DA Oct. 21 OU	

WAR DIARY
or
INTELLIGENCE SUMMARY.
(Erase heading not required.)

Army Form C. 2118.

D.A.D.O.S. 2nd Divn.

Place	Date	Hour	Summary of Events and Information	Remarks and references to Appendices
LA CROIX	1/4/17		Great difficulty experienced in clearing Batteries from last dump of Infantry, have left in storage until fresh Train is again imposed. The item objected to appeared to be put to clearance of Rations which is in great request by my Corn[?] team. Interior for the Fm. & Mess Synan Cain. Large demands from units for steel protective GS. Waynhund. Called 4 Im General Hilary M.T. Shops. Units afford Centre has been supplied as of any urgent. Prof Q+ Gurls unsaf[?] for mud. Weather conditions very demands have to be made in Pt. Bai in Ergonques. Been round to General further round [?] M. Bulk stone on by tty in Stem dimension, mineral & Industries for Flanville (Book[?]+Pommy SD. Batty + waterial) until further Muschiel. d Waffa Cant received at Radden for this Div. Am impelled to have my dumps(above 7 mile in time of most) stirring to fronties of Rodden & [?] of house. I want beimpossible to clear afterread Mounin.	

WAR DIARY
or
INTELLIGENCE SUMMARY
(Erase heading not required.)

Army Form C. 2118.

Place	Date	Hour	Summary of Events and Information	Remarks and references to Appendices
LA CAUCHIE	7/4/17		1.— Carriage 4.5 How. 1 — 4.5 How + Cartridge Empties + 1 — 18 Pr. in Cartridge Elements from Gun Park were destroyed by I.O.M. & the letter was shown to Commandant in S.P.A., but in hopes of their formation of Station. Reported position munitions to ADC III Corps. Arrange with Rt. to filler Guns & Carriages from Gun Park by Lorry instead of Team less Pert thru. 9.20 Ricochets in 9.45 T.M. received. Establish Advanced Dumps at Berelieux in Mint/ of Ambn. from Milliand Siere park. As besin of Gun in Tion/Been Another C. hires it is necessary fire to sustain the Carrier dump in Centre. Visit George Dumps. Arrival O/c to ensure last tin from in List Express — 4th released by him. 6.500 Ankle Amn, demanded to replace Batts FR. Army hmmn hmmn Imp from S. Demanded Ann To 3792. Dir. PF 4 creepy Chilled IRO. 76 & published in matter here which asep's drafts to return of known orders.

WAR DIARY
or
INTELLIGENCE SUMMARY.
(Erase heading not required.)

Army Form C. 2118.

Place	Date	Hour	Summary of Events and Information	Remarks and references to Appendices
W CAVEMNE	19/4/17		Orders to Sqn being taken up South of Bordeaux. There has W. L. Clement fun Achei le Grand. Marches from Tarets on Foot for Bordeaux & many Nos of horses missing. Una Cavalo reported at Bombay Ord Depot referring to my Carvin being employed chiefly collecti' material for Gun Park was unable to clear in time & Trickets were returned to Asyphet. Quan C, R.T.O. have my Gen to Bordeaux.	
BOI L Z UX -AC-MAT			Demand from 1st E. Yorks Regt for 12 Lewis Guns to replace Lost in action Supplied fr Gun Park when in charge of Withers & Culpet Ord Ret 2nd Reserve for men may be returned for mounting (Surveyed Horse & remounts) & their horses off led by army. 2050 Lost Saddle arrived from Gun Park Issued to meet immediate requirements of units returning from action. Large parade of Kits from Scherge — 1000 sets of funnel Leshoers — Gostle bay 4 Thermometers of suffar 30 for chem for men The Snell Cases & leather harness of Generals returned to Stores	

WAR DIARY
or
INTELLIGENCE SUMMARY.
(Erase heading not required.)

Army Form C. 2118.

Place	Date	Hour	Summary of Events and Information	Remarks and references to Appendices
BAPLEUX EN HONT	29/4/17		Quiet Day. Preparations in substitution of elements for Lewis & Hotchkiss from Spares Magazines etc. Large quantities of Magazines for Lewis from Reserve Equipment to enable Infantry to change Coy.	

30/4/17

W Morris
Cpl. I.O.
7 C.L.B.
H.Q.

CONFIDENTIAL.

A. 1187.

To:-

    D. A. G.,

        G.H.Q., 3rd Echelon.

With reference to your C.R., No. 140/452 of the 28th ult, herewith War Diary of the D.A.D.O.S., 21st Division, for the month of May 1917 as requested.

H.Q., 21st Div.,
11th July, 1917.

                       Major-General,
           Commanding 21st Division.

DADOS
Army Form C. 2118
2nd Divn.
Vol 20
31

WAR DIARY
or
INTELLIGENCE SUMMARY
(Erase heading not required.)

Place	Date	Hour	Summary of Events and Information	Remarks and references to Appendices
BOISLEUX AU MONT	1/5/17		Visit Brigades Comprising that many of the Stores Key in cellars upon to carry any of late value (title of this it am urgently required of in unfrequent quantity and furnished. In view of above arrangements are made for Battns to send to the Castle of Chipindale items contained in their S.103 Jr. the names of these was Chardhard + Signalling the nail items known to all commanders were Grosshard + Signalling Poles + Pegs. A Cage van of Knotts Type funds carrier is urgently asked for + a Magnesium of rams of Rear Bay + Resisters Type. This in lieu of eye wash. Lecce Punches of Voortin Born in France prohibited. Arranged with ADSsl Dr Corps for issuing of Peelthalin, chargers, Ammunition, Carrier + Aston	
	2/5/17			

WAR DIARY
or
INTELLIGENCE SUMMARY
(Erase heading not required.)

Army Form C. 2118

Place	Date	Hour	Summary of Events and Information	Remarks and references to Appendices
BorSLEUX AU MONT	15/7/17		Unable to provide Divisible Tools for Ammunition Dumps for D. A. C. by L.P. der from work at light Railways. Arrange through Engineers at Brigade Hdqrs for the return of all British Ammn except 1 Gun Brigade to Ammunition Dumps having been established in the area at The Circuse no. at Onellen. In Div. Laundry. Investigation + Scarcity of clothing is returned to Base for washing being unsatisfactory. As a Corps Laundry is short, Q to Corps notified before disposition is made. As a Camp at the Div. washing at Amiens be named arrangements are made to carry on. locker boxes + haversacks. All Ammunition Dumps supplies with heavier brenes + haversacks. Arrange with Snr. S.O. to supply point giving a camouflage effect in can of paint. Person Colom for Artilly units. This is essential if shelter is suppl. of J.C. Parnel.	
	31/5/17			

W. Grenier
Capt. ADMS

WAR DIARY or INTELLIGENCE SUMMARY
(Erase heading not required.)

Army Form C. 2118

D.A.D.O.S. 21st Division Vol 21

Place	Date	Hour	Summary of Events and Information	Remarks and references to Appendices
BOTTLEUX AU MONT	1/6/17		Question of return of Bullen Drawers & rain during summer months of hot weather is been discussed with A.D.O.S. Approximate numbers prepared to effect the change as regards Blankets, Shirts furnished to Corps. Arrange to obtain average return during Summer Months in returns of Corps demands covering period concerned. Purchased 200 lbs Dubbin owing to shortage in supplies from Base. Engaged in a new method of carrying spare cars to the Inspection by 1st Divisional Regt. forwarded to Corps. Routine duties.	
"	2/6/17			

WAR DIARY
or
INTELLIGENCE SUMMARY
(Erase heading not required.)

Army Form C. 2118

Place	Date	Hour	Summary of Events and Information	Remarks and references to Appendices
BOUZEUX 13 - AU - MONT	27/9/17		Attend Court of Enquiry at Archives C. Spans re loss of Stores Received from to April 24th Through offlowing Trucks & not unloading & spoons. R.T.O. Render Verdict. Arrange for Men to two of Germans Convicts - Dust Card & Rest Respecti- to further to be demanded & temporary to be returned to Stores. Collar &Ties of Stores from receives in fields for Stores. W Mann Capt RACH 21 CM.	

Army Form C. 2118.

Instructions regarding War Diaries and Intelligence Summaries are contained in F. S. Regs., Part II. and the Staff Manual respectively. Title Pages will be prepared in manuscript.

WAR DIARY
or
INTELLIGENCE SUMMARY
(Erase heading not required.)

D.A.D.O.S.
2nd Division

Vol 2

Place	Date	Hour	Summary of Events and Information	Remarks and references to Appendices
BONLEUX -AU- MONT.	1/7/17		Officers (F-9) (56 Div.) much wish to move our Bodies in rear of Sheets (in rest) of Paint. No sheets available at Corps or Army Dumps in Amiens Dep of Vickers & Lewis Guns at Arrangements made for Brixton in Amiens respectively. Those of 1 & 4 pdr. dull respectively. G.S. per Clarence reved. Le Cateau for deposit in Camp of this unit. Recommend that Brass & Bol of Beam suggested as an addition to Beams Equipment of Carpenters Tools is deficiency/any repairs likely to be carried out by unit.	
"	5/7/17		Visit thru Gysny Bryant Hargus, W.O.'s 1107 Rds. skin forwarded to 2nd Echelon Co my dump of such articles as Saucers Curriers (horse-gent port) etc. The return to my dump of such lauvenick Stores in Corps Area Salvage Dumps I rec'd	
"	7/7/17		Obtaining of elements in BATN. Visit dep'l Ordnance Dieppe & Camps were LOM. in repair of Machines of E.P. & G.S. Sectional Defencies.	

2449 Wt. W14957/M90 750,000 1/16 J.B.C. & A. Form/C.2118/12.

WAR DIARY
or
INTELLIGENCE SUMMARY

Army Form C. 2118.

Place	Date	Hour	Summary of Events and Information	Remarks and references to Appendices
BAILLEUL AU - MONT	8/7/17		Arrange with Infy Bde. re keeping Armourers with Bns. in Class Town with Divl Armourer Shop so that any parts available from Inf. Bde. Could open Divn. armoury.	
	12/7/17		Confer with L.O.M. i/c to measure of Carpenter Tools for in Lys Batts. To effect repairs & miscellaneous repairs. Suggest that R.E. workmen keep when II Army 0/45 issued to interpret. Whilst A.O.M. i/c Tailorness, Bootmender & Rains. Unable to locate Bns. in Twos in Lorry of Batts differed to retain. Suggest to unit the R.E. Coys if Bn. group might concur. Views. C/c II Army Gun. Park i Confer will hum 400 50 businesses of Armoury. Machines Gun & Sports & Collection of Stores separately. Return Issued to Posts no Bns have made a Chuptrack return.	
	17/7/17			

WAR DIARY
or
INTELLIGENCE SUMMARY
(Erase heading not required.)

Army Form C. 2118.

Place	Date	Hour	Summary of Events and Information	Remarks and references to Appendices
WULVERGHEM	18/7	11 PM	Capt. W.E.L. Lewis proceeded on Capt. Wilkin's conference of A.D.M.S. VIII Corps. Divisional Direction? Bringing in heads from hospital. Re G.R.O. 2448.	
		1 P.M.	Conference with Ten. M.O.M. HEND ECOURT regarding Tentage requested for by Nat Officer but includes to 21st Division. 21st Div. trunk requiring Part in that area will not include them in total return from thence. More notified.	
		6 P.M.	No 237 Machine Gun Coy joined the Battn from there. Water fatigue down Borders + selected area to erect reservoirs or M.D. Room.	
	19/7	3:30 PM	Visited 151St, 1/62 R.F.A. also 38 A.S.C. to Canal Footage and Report received F.R.S.M. VIII Corps remaining in position. Hostel still sniping, wire.	
		7 PM	Went on Weekly Telegraph + released	
			Letter to be met orderly.	
	20/7	?	Took over 21st Div. Ambulance area + transports from Capt. L. Miller 15 PM? who left for duty with VII Corps Laundry. VII Corps to purchase Lamps for Divisional ambulance, for A and D Corps to purchase either on payment - civil work, also lamps or deposit for rent trenches + hurdles from foul lands and supports to carriers.	

Army Form C. 2118.

WAR DIARY
or
INTELLIGENCE SUMMARY
(Erase heading not required.)

Instructions regarding War Diaries and Intelligence Summaries are contained in F. S. Regs., Part II. and the Staff Manual respectively. Title Pages will be prepared in manuscript.

Place	Date	Hour	Summary of Events and Information	Remarks and references to Appendices
BOIS L'EVÊQUE nr MONT	21/7/17	8 AM	Proceeded to Amiens & purchased Sketch books when returning routine work.	
	22/7/17		Visited HQ VII Corps & obtained 1100 francs for Inf. pay. S. Cattleau.	
	23/7/17	3 PM	Payment of Amount and requisition from 5 YW AS XIV Corps. S Cattleau Anti. Amm. move to H.Q. XIV Corps for inspection duty. Visited 12th & 13th MOUNTED BRIGADES with their troops Ammunition in connection with examination of Lewis guns & Anti-aircraft guns. Q. M.S. stores visited, no stock of stores or Clothing seen. Routine work. Arranger visit but Blve for inspection of Lewis guns & 12th & 13th Regts. 15 DL.J & 16 HOH.J on 25.7.17. Visited VII Corps and arrange demonstration	
			+ detailed Lewis gun parts for review.	
	24/7/17	11 AM	Bn visited by Afrd VII Corps. conferred subsequently out of arrangements for RFA - Previous reports to Hdqt. drawing up lists chap to 4 Army to examine Lewis guns & 9 KOYLI + 5th MGC on 26th. 3 armourer detailed to examine Rifles & ranges. Plate hits Bn with after a turn in the trenches. commencing 26-7-17 for 3 days.	

2449 Wt. W14957/M90 750,000 1/16 J.B.C. & A. Forms/C.2118/12.

WAR DIARY or INTELLIGENCE SUMMARY

Army Form C. 2118.

Place	Date	Hour	Summary of Events and Information	Remarks and references to Appendices
BOISLEUX AU MONT	25/1/17	10:30 AM	Visited 6th W. Yorks. the Lewis & armourers to view straining material for the tank in use. Arrangements for class from Divisional & visit 18 York. Rgt. 15 A.T.S. 1 n.m. 10/1/17 on 25th inst. - Continued with	
	26/1/17	10:30 AM	Visited 2 officer 6th J. Brrs. & conferred re extract exam's application in the Trenches – result satisfactory.	
		2 PM	Visited 14005 VII Corps in connection with defective M.G. barrels on Charge of Co. M.G. Coys. The rifles being corroded match will each be examined. Lewis Gunners runners for used for firing at Aeroplanes. Brock bombs not Sul. ammo also to last illumination rounds. Visited Corken VII Corps + Lieut. For trainees & repairs.	
	27/1/17	2 PM	Visited A.S.I. in 21 APS to examine defective rifles. Routine work.	
	28/1/17	10:30 AM	Visited 18 W.Y. (O.) all Lewis guns & their travel straps for overhaul. Visited H.Q. 62 Bgde re T. 14 & 5.3 Mark SVS. & coy in the carriage & parts of Hotchkiss Lewis gun in the remaining two brigades	

Army Form C. 2118.

WAR DIARY
or
INTELLIGENCE SUMMARY
(Erase heading not required.)

Instructions regarding War Diaries and Intelligence Summaries are contained in F. S. Regs., Part II. and the Staff Manual respectively. Title Pages will be prepared in manuscript.

Place	Date	Hour	Summary of Events and Information	Remarks and references to Appendices
Sept Camp Mont...	28/7/17	—	3 Armrs retd. from Inspection duty. Routine work. 15 Tents E.P.S. received from VIII Corps (in reorganisation of 25/P. W. Coy).	
	29/7/17	12.10 P.M.	Dump visited by A.D.O.S. VIII Corps. Indents were gone through. A.O.S. not satisfied with numbers of outstanding indents for pistols to replace casualties losses. Question taken up with A.O.S. re return to agg. strength. True Pistols taken off men admitted to field Ambce. - with a view to lessening demands on Base.	
	30/7/17		Routine work.	
	31/7/17	7 P.M.	Visited H.Q. Div. Routine work. Empty K.D. reserve retrieved. Off. leave, and recovered clothing on dand at 216...	

Wormwr Cyr...
ORD.O. 2.10 P.M

2449 Wt. W14957/M90 750,000 1/16 J.B.C. & A. Forms/C.2118/12.

Army Form C. 2118.

D.A.D.O.S.
21st Division
Vol 2 3

WAR DIARY
or
INTELLIGENCE SUMMARY
(Erase heading not required.)

Instructions regarding War Diaries and Intelligence Summaries are contained in F. S. Regs., Part II. and the Staff Manual respectively. Title Pages will be prepared in manuscript.

Place	Date	Hour	Summary of Events and Information	Remarks and references to Appendices
BORDEAUX AU MONT.	1/8/17. 3/8/17		Visited 1.O.M. 13/14 DAGp and arranged Programme for overhaul of Travelling Kitchens. Three Class experts of Field Ambulances & Divining Station Inspected return to m of Canadian equipment. Arranged for repairing return to m of Canadian. Brewers & Tanners from of Brewers Camp & returned to Ptarte. Brewers & returned to Creation. Conferences w C.O. Quartermaster & Brewers typed, journals of the necessity of reducing amount of surplus articles to a minimum. Arranged with I.O.M. 13/14 Dep for overhaul of dangers supplied Thick ties on Q.S. Finished Depm.	

Army Form C. 2118.

WAR DIARY
or
INTELLIGENCE SUMMARY
(Erase heading not required.)

Instructions regarding War Diaries and Intelligence Summaries are contained in F.S. Regs., Part II. and the Staff Manual respectively. Title Pages will be prepared in manuscript.

Place	Date	Hour	Summary of Events and Information	Remarks and references to Appendices
BOILEUX AU MONT	7/8/17		Visit of expert this week was P.D. Conroy has to be intimated for to explain how with war material constants for captain representative fuelled he unnecessary. Arranges this I will (supply) a certain amount of material for closing being done to Bn in Chg. But parts of these the downwards Ablyh from the River observation of Trenches that upper part of shen on beyond Nypois of then.	
"	19/8/17		Arrangements of 127? & 132? B.Ins: Northumberland Fusiliers. Arriving to utilize Trophium in manner to prevent is caused interesting interest in Bus. Conference of Belmont with AD & II Corps. Maj Gen Paul & Allward & Deacon hutri resp. II Army.	

2449 Wt. W14957/M90 750,000 1/16 J.B.C. & A. Forms/C.2118/12.

WAR DIARY or INTELLIGENCE SUMMARY

Army Form C. 2118

Place	Date	Hour	Summary of Events and Information	Remarks and references to Appendices
BOUZLEUX AU MONT	14/8/17		Lieut Anwary Orgames at Moyenneville. Miss Lieut Clay Bryn of Bombay an hand and orders Regt in of Commandity Painted to Battalion from Troops could be placed at hour disposal in guring Tom leave intact. Any Tin. 1/K Batln. changes to f on this Battalion of ince being an interval changes Bligr. Bn. Re-Arr.	
	20/8/17		Visit Duncan + orders change Tim. Return of equipment of Tim Yeomany Regts begun in being distributed. Army asks for permission of D.A.Q. to charge Tim S.A.A. Cart for Tim Gif. Federent Defence (Indian) Brigade Through Amalgamation by 12/7 + 13/9 Batt's horrhuntated Indian Comman granted of Bn. Carts + thirteen reserved Supplies returned to Base.	
BOUZEAUX	26/8/17		Move to Duncan + hand over my charge of Brigade un him to Dson 16/7 Div.	

Army Form C. 2118.

WAR DIARY
or
INTELLIGENCE SUMMARY
(Erase heading not required.)

Place	Date	Hour	Summary of Events and Information	Remarks and references to Appendices
BRISANE	27/8/17		Visit Brigade HQrs. Routine duties.	
	31/8/17		Arranged to train Brown to carry on Armourers to carry on with duties upon return to Shier Regiment. Armourer is doing duty in Bde ARMRS Shop.	

Mcframin
Capt DAPCM
21 RW

WAR DIARY
or
INTELLIGENCE SUMMARY

(Erase heading not required.)

Army Form C. 2118

WO 95 2125 Vol 25

Place	Date	Hour	Summary of Events and Information	Remarks and references to Appendices
DUISANS	1/9/17		Divisional Artillery less Division in II Army area minus Seven Guns. Army, Corps + Divnl SgtS on holyday. Visit Brigade HeadQrs re special Stores required under from Kaysen conditions in held area. All Batteaulay supplies to their return in Mot Lor Lake returned to be returned to XVIII Corps before leaving this area. Visit ADVA XVII Corps. has Type of Canvas Carrier for Rifle Grenades is being tried by Six Rifle Grenades resting h.e. Good apparently. He carries Tank. Six Grenades + Steel Circlets to take the Stem of the Grenade. My Scheme is Carrier to be carried by with Chago Cover + Shrovels when fired in occurred to Corpls respect.	

WAR DIARY
INTELLIGENCE SUMMARY
(Erase heading not required.)

Army Form C. 2118.

Place	Date	Hour	Summary of Events and Information	Remarks and references to Appendices
DU(LAN)	9/9/17		New method of carrying down from country of corrugated strip (wicker) both beth ring to carry myself but — left the Bruins to carry Bruifers. Being made up in P.W. from salvaged material chips. Infant being is made up. Armoured strip to the base of the slide Jan. "Carry" plates. Carriers to be sent Prohibited made up by me. Three of Regt obtained from R.E. + Engrs personnel roads.	
"	12/9/17		Visit dear Mother Bishop. Abouri.re (Intestinale) never flu. Rain in morn. Home to Canteen II Army Corps.	
CAESTRE	15/9/17		Visit A.D.M.S X Corps & D.A.D.H. 39th Divn. re hy R.F.A. personnel up training too. Visit Heavy Mobile Workps II Army.	

Army Form C. 2118.

WAR DIARY
or
INTELLIGENCE SUMMARY
(Erase heading not required.)

Instructions regarding War Diaries and Intelligence Summaries are contained in F. S. Regs., Part II. and the Staff Manual respectively. Title Pages will be prepared in manuscript.

Place	Date	Hour	Summary of Events and Information	Remarks and references to Appendices
CAESTRE	19/9/17.		Visit Calais Base depot to collect Tepi repeatedly represented by WOST for Infantry return. Find is up to full War Tables. Application for an observer of this material in a cheaper constitute for an Infantry Battalion forwarded under Terms of G.R.O. 11331.	
	21/9/17		Cow ACH & Corps & arrangement to carry be made in II Army for the supply of Cartridge Expansive for 3" Stokes Guns in in II Army.	
			2nd DIVL Artillery Arrangement been to take from March 3q 9 cm.	
	22/9/17		Visit ACM I Corps concerning question of Gun Roses for Div. R.F.A. and II Army Machine Gun Base. Spread have between Riffe Grenade Comm is made up from material (Cannon) supplied by me to Contractors.	

Army Form C. 2118.

WAR DIARY
or
INTELLIGENCE SUMMARY
(Erase heading not required.)

Instructions regarding War Diaries and Intelligence Summaries are contained in F.S. Regs., Part II. and the Staff Manual respectively. Title Pages will be prepared in manuscript.

Place	Date	Hour	Summary of Events and Information	Remarks and references to Appendices
CAESTRE	23/9/17		Arrange with Divisions 41st Divn & 39 Divn re precision stores for two from Machine Gun Stores for my units in forward area. Machine Gun Officers consulted re ammunition, complete spare parts with spare Sets that Coys are not really receiving.	
METEREN	23/9/17		Move to Meteren. L.P. of P. Tabbs for laundry has made ADMS return. Also 18 Chairs. Provision of Manufacture in Divl ARMOURERS SHOP. Items reqd. of Tools for previous ammunition boxes for D.A.C.	
"	29/9/17		Visit ADH. D Corps re extra allotment of Kilts Cinders & dressing gowns.	
"	30/9/17			

Wyham
Capt. DADOS
21 Divn.

2449 Wt. W14957/M90 750,000 1/16 J.B.C. & A. Forms/C.2118/12.

WAR DIARY
or
INTELLIGENCE SUMMARY

Army Form C. 2118

DADOS.
31st Divison

Vol 25

Place	Date	Hour	Summary of Events and Information	Remarks and references to Appendices
MICMAC CAMP near Ouderdom	1/10/17		L.P. of Cmd for Ypres Front — 10 yards per Rest — receiving depot. Ascertain Gen'l in [illegible]. Saw Machine Gun Officer Obtain 100 Bands for Vickers guns from Corps Machine Gun Officer. Visit A.D.T. & Engrs.	
"	3/10/17		Division Pioneers instead no. in Bivs & Camps — When reinforced no. has been upset as at morning — wire I.O.M. & R.E.O. Open an Advanced Dump at Advanced Div. Hqrs. to deal specially with "Battle" in specially letter attd.	
"	5/10/17		Demand for attd. for men joining Divn. A.D.T. on leaving join of Special Orders to Receiving divisn.	

Army Form C. 2118.

WAR DIARY
or
INTELLIGENCE SUMMARY
(Erase heading not required.)

Instructions regarding War Diaries and Intelligence Summaries are contained in F.S. Regs., Part II. and the Staff Manual respectively. Title Pages will be prepared in manuscript.

Place	Date	Hour	Summary of Events and Information	Remarks and references to Appendices
BLARINGHEM	8/15/17		Move from MICMAC CAMP to BLARINGHEM. Vis. Rackent, Machine Gun Stores & Light Workshops. With 6 Batteries Temporarily stationed in Your area whilst Div. horses in the days time arrangements are made for him to inspect them to ensure proper maintenance by R.F.A. Change in this area as a demonstration centre. Impossible to obtain troops & Protection from Bar.	
	12/1/17		Visit A.D.M.S. & Cages. Private elected O, Cages. I. for my change at N1 central Shelter it life. Elected O, Cages. I (for pennsion of ambulance). Chosen my own Inspection from to be in forenoon of MICMAC. Chateau Signal (near Div. Hayes) and MICMAC.	
	15/1/17		10 Delivered distin O, Cages. Div. in F'nn of the him to him been made arrangements on hasten with Cages for their return to Rug season. Repl. Attle.	

WAR DIARY or INTELLIGENCE SUMMARY

Army Form C. 2118

Place	Date	Hour	Summary of Events and Information	Remarks and references to Appendices
BLARINGHEM	19/10/17		Visit Bty Captains & their Sergeants Bdrs & Officers representing for return to Bde.	
CHATEAU SEGARD. YPRES	23/10/17		Orders 2 Telescope Rflrs from Empire School. Munston Capt. F.S. Batt Drivers Bullen & Veste. Demand furniture for F.S. Batt to Ordnance Depot in Ypres.	
"	24/10		Move from Blaringhem to Chateau Segard 237 Divl Rte met minister for an advance dump led by command in most. Flight of 303 from from Pacific Thigh from forward dump Army areas works on early days to be in reserve. Band of Box Respirator from Paroh 14:30 to Reserve 1 mortar fresh to Begnigton.	
"	25/10/17		Respirator returned to 147 Div.	
"	31/10/17		39th Div. R.F.A. moved to the Div.	

M.G.? Capt RAAH
21 Div.

14   21
Army Form C. 2118.

DADOS 31st Division

Vol 26

WAR DIARY
or
INTELLIGENCE SUMMARY.
(Erase heading not required.)

November 1917

Place	Date	Hour	Summary of Events and Information	Remarks and references to Appendices
CHATEAU SEGARD (YPRES)	1/11/17		Visit sub dump at MICHAELCAMP also Railhead at OUDERDOM. Arrange for six extra fatigue men to report to Young Dump. Arrange for unexpired return Div. for ammunition parties to S.E. of Ypres. Less Rifle Grenade Cartridges.	
"	5/11/17	10M	W.5 & 5th Brit Brigp (Inft) refuse to accept 5 carriages complete. C/94 R.F.A asked to be held to evacuate him for them. Carriages had to be partly evacuated — Rest them in Brigde & Sixty sudden them. Proceeded this hasten. 1st H.Q.W. & Corps.	
"	6/11/17	08.27	Further batteries at 11.50 Ammunition to be received from Front Dump. G.O.R. Gun Wipers & Sites for his L.O. Clothing Bags. Very urgent.	
			Area to be cleared to Infantry whilst Witnesses for the ?	
"	7/11/17		Brig Genl & S ? taking by various visitors & Gen Clarke.	
"	8/11/17		Visit new areas of select site for dump.	

Army Form C. 2118.

WAR DIARY
or
INTELLIGENCE SUMMARY.
(Erase heading not required.)

Place	Date	Hour	Summary of Events and Information	Remarks and references to Appendices
CHATEAU DE GRAND (YPRES)	13/4/17		Change to Camp near Rope S.E. unnamed farm my plan to say am. 300 On Outer received from Base. Discussing with AOMS question of Technical equipment & stores from Au Post of Divism Artil. Total Great number to Field Ambulances. Commence in Rin.	
	14/4/17		New HOME II Corps & Corps RH Hinga a Henry own to 20 Anyac Corps. Trying of all outstanding me wp for Him & Ccavys of 21 Dr. & RFT F.F. Brett received from Base on [?] II Hope as [?] is awarded. Hiny of them also on my [?] on an. I've two representatives to AOM I Corps.	
VIEUX BERQUIN	16/4/17		Move Office to Vieux Berquin.	
BERLIN	18/4/17		Move office & dumps to BERLIN.	

WAR DIARY
or
INTELLIGENCE SUMMARY.
(Erase heading not required.)

Army Form C. 2118.

Place	Date	Hour	Summary of Events and Information	Remarks and references to Appendices
BERLIN	19/11/17		Accept. invit. to Bn. Rathen. BERLIN.	
			Morn. tour of 76, 62nd Div. G. Corp. as they were to form res. tomorrow.	
			Visit 2nd Army Purr. Res HERSIN & team coy of from her then	
			Visit AOH 1st Corps, OOH 1st Army on forming 2nd Cav. Div by Siv.	
	29/11/17		Visit OAOH 47 Div. Lt Channel ARRAS & arranges statem. num from his	
			Visit AOH XIII Corps & discuss position & dispositn. of Div. Res. in	
			Corps Area re.	
	24/11/17		Visit HQ Corps 21st Div. Arty. LA AGZ.	
			2 Corps Artillerie destroyed by LA Corps. HEREIN. Bay for reg.	
G CHARLAINE 24			them to ARRAS reinforcing	
ARRAS	11/17		Confrnce c/ AOH XIII Corp. offic. are equipping of 21st Artillery.	
			All Reg/t Capt. & OAOH & Corps present	

WAR DIARY
or
INTELLIGENCE SUMMARY.

(Erase heading not required.)

Army Form C. 2118.

Place	Date	Hour	Summary of Events and Information	Remarks and references to Appendices
N. CATHERINE			Conference at Div. ARTY. Hqrs. re retiral positions to rear of BAPAUME	
A.R.H.Q.	25/11/17		The Division being under Orders to proceed shortly to another theatre of war, Transfer is to take place in stages & enquiries are made.	
"	28/11/17		Advance party "D" & Garrison of each Ammunition for Divisions	
"	29/11/17		leave to ITALY. Colonel & men went to proceed to PERONNE area	
			Head qtr. & A. Comm. I. Comn. are party in charge of Corps Comdg. of Gunns accumulated to rear of here to ITALY. Despatch Bicycles returned by Divl. Artillery Cnn. of here to Base.	
"	30/11/17		Arrived TINCOURT. VII Corps area	

Major Cpt. DSOM
2iC ON

Army Form C. 2118.

DADDS 2nd Division

Vol 27

WAR DIARY
or
INTELLIGENCE SUMMARY
(Erase heading not required.)

Instructions regarding War Diaries and Intelligence Summaries are contained in F. S. Regs., Part II. and the Staff Manual respectively. Title Pages will be prepared in manuscript.

Place	Date	Hour	Summary of Events and Information	Remarks and references to Appendices
TINCOURT	2/12/17		Move dump from St. Catherine ARRAS to TINCOURT. As no arrangement for a dump there been made the 4 Lorries are kept loaded overnight.	
	3/12/17		On arrival in VII Corps area Genl. FOSTER in Bed praising of dump. TOISEL is Dugented & visited by me. "Accept" iron hut lent to Brar.	
	4/12/17		The length of our stay not being known only such items as Gen Appleham require & spares rouern are for the present brought from Cat owen.	
	5/12/17		All bicycles rendered Irregalvo by change in R.F.A. Units of Divring Armn for bicycles are returned to Brar except those wanted to meet outstanding indents.	
	6/12/17		Attend Conference of officer of ADOS. VII Corps.	

WAR DIARY
or
INTELLIGENCE SUMMARY

Army Form C. 2118.

Papers 21 Div 1917

Place	Date	Hour	Summary of Events and Information	Remarks and references to Appendices
ROISEL	8/12/17		Special visit to Bde heavy to obtain Cy comm Garage for magazines in Amm Dump & further supply of tools for general ammunition boxes.	
"	9/12/17		Battery to have precautions taken to clean transport is used to clean milked.	
"			Called 2nd Tauranteers from Cyps TP. he Brayonne & Spr Battles having been taken over in this dist Sgt. TP Ashwood each one demanded from Bm. Lieut. Knapp North Regt arrived from Drony 2nd TP.Bm. for attachment to be d. inspector.	
"	13/12/17	2— 7.45	Trence Mortars received & Reviewed	
"	14/12/17		Suggested scale of issue of electric torches submitted to D.A.D.Q	

Army Form C. 2118.

WAR DIARY
or
INTELLIGENCE SUMMARY

(Erase heading not required.)

Instructions regarding War Diaries and Intelligence Summaries are contained in F. S. Regs., Part II. and the Staff Manual respectively. Title Pages will be prepared in manuscript.

Place	Date	Hour	Summary of Events and Information	Remarks and references to Appendices
POISEL	15/12/17	—	Capt R. Browne + Lt V. G. Knapp (attached) proceeded on leave. 400 Bayonets + 500 Rattles received from Base. 2300 Gum Boots Thigh received from 24th divn.	
"	16/12/17	—	4000 pprs Socks received to complete Reserve of 5000	
"	17/12/17	—	Routine work	
"	18/12/17	—	Visited ADOS VII Corps for Conference. Received instructions from 2nd Army to come into line with other divisions of VII Corps + was at B129 for Brock to come into line from 1-1-18 requirements in return of the Brock Powder sheets. Visited OC VII Corps Troops for GS white sand— These had not been received from Base. Collected one Vickers gun for 2 MG Coy from the 3 Grn PWK, Albert. Owing to heavy fall of snow on 17th great difficulty was experienced in travelling.	
"	19/12/17	—	Routine work	
"	20/12/17	—	Visited VII Corps Troops OQ + Collected 65 snow suits & 40 Rifle Covers. Also 5200 fire from Crosois, together a new firing in lower + purchase material (FD 9 r).	

Army Form C. 2118.

WAR DIARY
or
INTELLIGENCE SUMMARY
(Erase heading not required.)

Instructions regarding War Diaries and Intelligence Summaries are contained in F. S. Regs., Part II. and the Staff Manual respectively. Title Pages will be prepared in manuscript.

Place	Date	Hour	Summary of Events and Information	Remarks and references to Appendices
ROISEL	21/12/17	—	Visited Corbie to purchase Xmas mails. There are rumours on byways with heavy hoar recognition, the wild bow important onwards towards	
	22/12/17	—	Office return. Visited by A.D.O.S. VII Corps, who gave indications for A.M.S. staff. Tailors shop, & Boot repairing shops to be established. Kilt & winter conditions. Received 2070 Green Envs. 1500 Forms from Canteen VIII Corps & 784 sets = 5848 set. Also I received from Bord.	
	23/12/17	—	GHQ ample Supplies of Xmas cheer & sports received from home also Xmas mails which were due, vide report of 21.12.17	
	24/12/17	—	Routine	
	25/12/17	—	Various festivities employed - inducted Xmas dinner for all ranks 9/20 received a large quantities notes ages 2921 - Report on same received 6/11/18	
	26/12/17 27/12/17	— —	Routine	

Army Form C. 2118.

WAR DIARY
or
INTELLIGENCE SUMMARY
(Erase heading not required.)

Instructions regarding War Diaries and Intelligence Summaries are contained in F. S. Regs., Part II. and the Staff Manual respectively. Title Pages will be prepared in manuscript.

Place	Date	Hour	Summary of Events and Information	Remarks and references to Appendices
ROISEL	28/12/17		Dispatched 1135 whizz bangs and to complete to 1st Bri S.T. VIII G @ 3030. Visited MERVILLE & paid a bill of 39 fr for the manufacture of Lewis Gun Covers.	
"	29/12/17		Routine. Pte Gidlow ATS joined for duty from HAVRE in relief of Pte Runcie.	
"	30/12/17	10.30 AM	Office strong visited by ASC VIII Corps. Received instructions to obtain part of the front Left reserve kit horse shoes & other arts in the unit so as to be in a position to meet urgent requirements in forward (or other) fronts.	
"	31/12/17		Capt: R.L. Quarrie MD. returned off leave over Xmas. & as Lt V.G. Knott Welch Regt. also MO. see Signed MKeane	

M Brennan Comdt
ASC

Army Form C. 2118.

WAR DIARY
or
INTELLIGENCE SUMMARY.
(Erase heading not required.)

DADOS 31st Division Vol 28
January 1918

Place	Date	Hour	Summary of Events and Information	Remarks and references to Appendices
ROISEL	1/1/18	1/1/18	"Accept" from To Bombat. Queries consulting of all outstanding indents w/ Div & units of organisation. Return To Camer. all except special items (GKC etc.) Visit L.O.M. to 93/47 Bde.	
	4/1/18	1/1/18	Visit III Army Gun Park (at Veecq). Arrange with Ord. re. establishing of Armour & C.G. Repair shops in winter quarters & in complete revision of known & voted Guns & Vehicles for proposed all armour equip 1 per Bde battalion & Brit. Lega	
7	6/1/18	1/1/18	Visit Bdes (Inf). Queries specialist & immediate Equipment announcements for Machine Gun etc. Complete show Gun only to Approved Arrange with D.M.T for delivery of Special Tools for Gunnery Armourers Exam.	
7	9/1/18	1/1/18	Confer 4/5 Aust. Field Col. Farrar on approval for temporary issue, and Visit Lient. Knapp (attached AOD) approves for temporary only and	

WAR DIARY
or
INTELLIGENCE SUMMARY.
(Erase heading not required.)

Army Form C. 2118.

Place	Date	Hour	Summary of Events and Information	Remarks and references to Appendices
ROISEL	15/4/18		Issued 400 Bouzers. Drew rather of Checks Tentage in Corps area with R.Q. 2-9.45" Trench Mortars received from Base at Railway. Forward 6 suspected Scarecrow cars of Elastic tenelar to Army Div. Issued 50 Bayers L.1000. Receive instructions to proceed in Ammunition Course Sho 14 Ord Depot.	
	12/1/18		Leave for No 14 Ord Depot.	

Wigram Capt RAVC
RION

WAR DIARY or INTELLIGENCE SUMMARY

(Erase heading not required.)

Army Form C. 2118.

Place	Date	Hour	Summary of Events and Information	Remarks and references to Appendices
ROISEL	12/5		Capt R L Duarrie proceeded to No 14 Ord: Depôt for a Course, vice 2/Lt E Army W/re M-11-7-18 C 2180 rue A X 3 F /11-1-18	
	13/8		Usual precautions taken. 2 G.S wagons yesterday to divs from No 673 Coy. 2/Lt Drew to replace lorries, four drivers employed in cleaning their vehicles, and one having in the lorry park, the village stables two double lined houses in the village.	
		8PM	Usual precautions resumed.	
	14/5	7 AM	2 Wagons got returned to Train.	
	15/5	10:30 AM	Attended Conference at Office 1/Lith VII Corps. Discussed question of issue of blankets to reinforcements - received GRO 266. Weather very warm, all day & rain in the evening - Two stables were damaged by the storm - detail subordinates supplements material by request. Usual precautions on for 8 pm	
	16/5	9AM	Two G.S wagons reported not to replace those lorries. 500 prs Gum boots thigh received from Cps IV Corps Troops.	

A6943 Wt. W14944/M1160 350,000 12/16 D. D. & L. Forms/C./2118/14

Army Form C. 2118.

WAR DIARY
or
INTELLIGENCE SUMMARY.
(Erase heading not required.)

Instructions regarding War Diaries and Intelligence Summaries are contained in F. S. Regs., Part II. and the Staff Manual respectively. Title pages will be prepared in manuscript.

Place	Date	Hour	Summary of Events and Information	Remarks and references to Appendices
ROISEL	17th		Routine	
	18th		Visited ADS, Gun Park + collected M.G. parts, also visited H.Q. 3 Div. Workshops to exchange cylinder for Alzander stove. Collect at Corps Salvage dump	
	19th	10.30am	Office + Sunt visited by ADOS VII Corps. Col K.J.B.S Goody outstanding indents gone through. discussed the question of tanks demanded by units for reinforcements in view of GRO 266	
		11.Am	Office-dump visited by ADOS VII Div. workshops	
	20th		Routine	
	21st	9.30am	Visited office of ADOS VII Corps to receive instructions regarding removal to in the Cordestration Camp about to be formed at ATHIES 12.00 D.R. from VII Corps Cashier for £100.4/0	
	22nd		100 Latrine Buckets } received from B.Ord 4n 21BSD at Cross Slates 200 Lamps Hurricane } to Headquarters by instruction against invoice Bomb. completed.	

WAR DIARY
or
INTELLIGENCE SUMMARY.
(Erase heading not required.)

Army Form C. 2118.

Place	Date	Hour	Summary of Events and Information	Remarks and references to Appendices
ROISEL	23/8	2.20pm	Visited 63rd Field Ambce & checked clothing - vide GRO 2921	
	24/8		Routine	
	25/8		Routine	
	26/8	8.40am	Visited VII Corps Salvage dump & collected & forwarding Flags	
			Delivered to Corps Notes Board to OO VII Corps George, Spethigere	
			& Jiment to Shop to Inspect Arms Gunfire an 3 stores	
			at No 3 Ombulahoppetn Office & Ind Vadois MASON VII Corps	
	27/8		Gone general stores received instructions received to	
			Overhaul & prepare for Hospital 100 Yards received from	
			Area Condr Peronne. Longinouis	
	28/8		Lieut Acct Supt of Armourer G.R. WAITE AOD returned from	
			Have Zythe Army for Temp duty	
	29/8		Lieut C. ROBERTS arrived for Temporary duty from VII Corps Troops	
		11.10am	Office & dump visited by A.D.O.W.R 2/8 Div	
		6.15pm	Captain R.S.Quionie returned from 14 Ord Depot and assumed	
			duty as DADOS 2/8 Div	

WABrennan Cond AOC

Army Form C. 2118.

WAR DIARY
or
INTELLIGENCE SUMMARY.
(Erase heading not required.)

Place	Date	Hour	Summary of Events and Information	Remarks and references to Appendices
ROUEN	30/1/18		Returned from Commanding Officers at No 14. Beyond. Lieut. T. Roberts A.D.C. wrote for Temporary attachments duty. Visit A.D.M.S. VII Corps.	
"	31/1/18		Am granted special leave to United Kingdom commencing 31st for seven days.	

Mgherin
Capt RAMC
3/1/18
21st Div

Army Form C. 2118.

WAR DIARY
or
INTELLIGENCE SUMMARY.
(Erase heading not required.)

DADOS
21st Division
Vol 29

January 1918.

Place	Date	Hour	Summary of Events and Information	Remarks and references to Appendices
ROISEL	1/1/18	11-15 AM	Capt. O'Quance proceeded on leave 3 Wks. Offie - dump visited by ADOS VII Corps. Receive order to attend Conference at 11-30 AM on 3-2-18 (Thursday)	
		4 PM	Visited OC VII Corps Troops & delivered 25 pull. pegs 15" dia. x 4½" dump notice. Orders received to visit ADOS AMG 21st Div on 2/2/17	
	2/1/17		Lieut. C. Roberts ATS left for duty as RTO ARRAS. Attended the some meeting by his Lord ship. In salvage & bicycle reports.	
			Repr. Bretancourt & Guilin moved into CMG Dumps - Orders of ADOS VII Corps. Visited AD AMG 21st Div. Returned to this office & made a few	
		11 AM	Schemes for personnel hire & MO returned & instructed as to procedure in dealing with receipts & disposal of stores. Arrangements made with RAO for Tinsmiths as required. Question of future duties applicable to 3/c Q.M.S & MDRgr & 10th Works Ry. Moved visit serial no. OS 4966 OS/SAL 273 M 29/1/17.	
	3/1/17	11.30 AM	Attended conference at ADOS VII Corps Office discussed questions of receiving and disposing of stores on Evacuation scheme.	
		2.30	A.M.O. Dumps to ADOS 2/2 Division. 7 two tone cars to ALL on Dump 2/1	

WAR DIARY or INTELLIGENCE SUMMARY

Army Form C. 2118.

(Erase heading not required.)

Instructions regarding War Diaries and Intelligence Summaries are contained in F. S. Regs., Part II. and the Staff Manual respectively. Title pages will be prepared in manuscript.

Place	Date	Hour	Summary of Events and Information	Remarks and references to Appendices
ROISEL	3/7/18	2pm	3/7 The Queens (Rwf) Regt. commenced surveys to MT. Eynde. Reserve at form 0.8.VIII. Boys Scouts and Telescope prisms not rected qual. for signs to SngO 21/8/18. Guts outfits stereoscopic given to Armn.	
	4/7/18	–	Issued Telescope to men with hosterl from to SngO. Visited I Div.	
			17th (X) bishops and attempted for park Kinnards to report. Shept for Lewis gun.	
	5/7/18	4PM	Office today visited by Brigadier VII Corps.	
		–	2nd Queens Regt. joined Div from MT.DIV. – Inv order rick para HQ Indian; to Oft circulates. 7/8/18 Queens (Regt) Regt – 10th Yorks Regt. moved Fontenoir vide notice OL 4966. 10 Kings and 2 Leinsts Regt moved vide notice OL 4967. On disbandment 10th Yorks Regt commenced landing in India in Egypt	
		3pm	3/7 The Queens returned their Rifles fitted with Telescope sights.	
	6/7/18	7pm	Received report of Progress in returning of Equipt by units affected	
		–	6000 sets knives/cutting received from GHQ VII Corps troops as per stock issues at Provisional Laundry.	

Army Form C. 2118.

WAR DIARY
or
INTELLIGENCE SUMMARY.
(Erase heading not required.)

Place	Date	Hour	Summary of Events and Information	Remarks and references to Appendices
ROISEL	6/2/18	1	Commenced a record of progress in the handing in of Equipt. Service received that cars Q.344 & 1/101 can be drawn from No 3 Gun Park. No transport available on 7th.	
	7/2/18		Delivered bend sets undertaking to 2nd Bath that Marie adviser to draw 2015 Vulcan Packs from O.D.V.III Corps troops to Corps H/S Bn. at 4:50 — Drawn 3pm. T.M. Coys. (Reg. No. 921) received from 21st T.M.B. Due 9.45am.	
			10h 45 y & I commenced handing in Equipment. Despatch One truck returned fr. Egypt. Chiefs supplies Equipt. Range finding stores w/ R-base Hayne. 16 Lewis guns complete delivered to 24th Army Gun Park, a/c ordnance on return by the Division	
	8/2/18	12:30pm	Capt R.L.Quentin returned to resume duty as Adjut. ~~~~~~~~~~~~~~~~~~~ McKernan Capt R.C.	

WAR DIARY
or
INTELLIGENCE SUMMARY.
(Erase heading not required.)

Army Form C. 2118.

Instructions regarding War Diaries and Intelligence Summaries are contained in F. S. Regs., Part II. and the Staff Manual respectively. Title pages will be prepared in manuscript.

Place	Date	Hour	Summary of Events and Information	Remarks and references to Appendices
ROISEL	9/2/18		Visit MG Companies re Exchange of Pistols for Rifles & return of same.	
			Visit Bn. HQrs & discuss return of stores of entrenching Infantry Materials.	
			15 Telescopic Sighted Rifles returned by car to V Army Inspn Depot.	
"	15/2/18		At entrance of QrMrStores:- raised questn of his Issue f rains of Electric Vaudhu.	
			Announcemts made re return of Pct. Helmets to Base	
			Visit ADOS VII Corps & discuss dispersal of 2nd Trench Mortars Co.	
			Referred for hires Transport to be attd to my permanent Trans Jerusalem.	
"	19/2/18		More announcemts with units re renewal of Cartridges from rifles	

A6945 Wt. W14442/M1160 350,000 12/16 D. D. & L. Forms/C./2118/14

WAR DIARY
or
INTELLIGENCE SUMMARY.
(Erase heading not required.)

Army Form C. 2118.

Place	Date	Hour	Summary of Events and Information	Remarks and references to Appendices
ROISEL	22/2/18		Forward suggested divisional reserve of First Corps to be held. Reg. me. 10 Cav ~ ½" Cyc + 5 Cav to 2nd Cyc. Visit Divis Red Station & cheque stock of cav. held there " 62nd + 64th Div. Hdqrs. Visit to 5 Divise Kopships (Henry) + Gm Pern h.q. 5. Attent expenses at Corps Hedqrs. Cord. Office.	
"	24/2/18		Visit Divis Stables & chosen industries excercis	
"	28/2/18			

W. Mann
Col. RAVC
21st Divn

WAR DIARY
or
INTELLIGENCE SUMMARY
(Erase heading not required.)

Army Form C. 2118.

DAHS 212

Place	Date	Hour	Summary of Events and Information	Remarks and references to Appendices
ROISEL	1/3/18		View Plan & R.E.O re removal of Cut offs from Bgde. Reorganisation of M.G. Coys. Drawn specification of framework construction at Corps experience. Reception of M.T. & M.T. Lewis Gunners for use with 2" Trench mortar Battery for close in-unit control in Divisional Ammunition Dump.	96.30
"	2/3/18		Command change of scene from B.H.Q. to Counter-Batteries experienced at last 5 heavy mortar Coys. Instruction carried out A.D.H to Coys covering Hostile from main T.S Standing Orders for A.A. Purposes. The main guns & gun positions & when shelled. Ample with 10 M Heavy Coys for 5 mins to be used.	
LONSAVESNES	22/3/18		Moved to LONSAVESNES.	
ST. DENIS	22/3/18		Moved from LONSAVESNES to ST. DENIS. Dump shelled all down dot. Reception of Corps Covering Charts.	
MARICOURT	23/3/18		Moved from ST. DENIS to MARICOURT. Dump moved there for S Corps. Two Corps Clerks here reporting Two Corps Stores taken for chewing dump.	

Army Form C. 2-18.

WAR DIARY
or
INTELLIGENCE SUMMARY.
(Erase heading not required.)

Place	Date	Hour	Summary of Events and Information	Remarks and references to Appendices
MARICOURT	24/3/18		Remove dump from MARICOURT to BRAY. All stores cleared. Sent to the S-gun Park for Horses & Lorries from & return to Div. HQrs. 6 Horses & 2 lorries.	
LA NEUVILLE	25/3/18		Offrs & dumps move to LA NEUVILLE. Obtain fresh supples of Rifle Oil & Flannelette to replenish reserve must to units. Ord; Lack stores in store room, Rifle Oil & Flannelette being reissued for Ben water carrying containers. 72 Very Pistols (1") demanded for Bde.	
ALLONVILLE	29/3/18		Visit CCS. encamped LA NEUVILLE. Clear CCS at LA NEUVILLE.	
"	31/3/18		Cartridges demand by units to Bde. for agreement in Transport, Lewis & Lewis gun Distribution to be bad on base of present strength.	

[signature]
Capt AAQM
21 Div

Army Form C. 2118.

DADOS
3rd Division
Vol 31

WAR DIARY
or
INTELLIGENCE SUMMARY.
(Erase heading not required.)

Place	Date	Hour	Summary of Events and Information	Remarks and references to Appendices
ALONVILLE	1/4/18		Moved Dump to CHEPSTRE. II Army new Visit A.D.O.S. Australian Corps re selection of new dump.	
PERNOIS	3/4/18		Large indents for returning received from units — sum of the principle. Amounts being (in fillers) — Bicycle. 165 Very Pistols. 181 Pickers fur. 48 Lenses " 51 + 60 + 47 S.L. Lamps. 4 A.G.S. " 102 Fuel Kitchens 14 Binoculars (prism) 87. (prism) 321 Prismatic Compass 57 Comp. Magnetic Pocket 287 Watches wrist 10	

WAR DIARY
or
INTELLIGENCE SUMMARY.
(Erase heading not required.)

Army Form C. 2118.

Place	Date	Hour	Summary of Events and Information	Remarks and references to Appendices
DRANOUTRE	7/4/18		Complete Transport (12 Vehicles) delivered on arrival at Billeting in return of G. Div. Had approximation to meet Transport. Considerable excess demand produced by units for Transport. Arrang'd to MTR ADSD to send in precis of any confusion existing within Div. Proceeded forward electric Toroidon to Hostain for Batt. Recommend to Div. Ship. Had application under terms of S.R.O. 1133 for an establishment of electric torches for M.S. BDE. be made. he return of present returned to AFC 10PB.	
DICKEBUSCH	10/4/18		Mr. RICKMAN whom now charge of ADMIN. 49 Div. Applied a line charge of Nelveton.	
"	11/4/18		Gave Charge over to BOESCHEPE. Arrang'd for all Infantry Transport in the Div. after reporting to be sent to be Charge of BOESCHEPE. Sheet Contained 72 Very Pistols returned from Bn units returning before to Corps be Cleared. Reported at ABORNIC 9. Sent to Corps.	

Army Form C. 2118.

WAR DIARY
or
INTELLIGENCE SUMMARY.
(Erase heading not required.)

Instructions regarding War Diaries and Intelligence Summaries are contained in F. S. Regs., Part II. and the Staff Manual respectively. Title pages will be prepared in manuscript.

Place	Date	Hour	Summary of Events and Information	Remarks and references to Appendices
DICKEBUSCH	12/4/18		Truck & Stores & AUDRUICQ. Cleared up for to provide by us lorry to transport Stores received to #3 ☒ ☐ ☐. (The Stores of #10 Truck to 28/4/18 a van sent to Stores in 5.B. disposed also to R.O. AUDRUICQ.)	
"	14/4/18		Cecil for lorry Crew & Gun Butts from pioneer area to cultivate. Officer & main dump moved to ABEELE.	
HOOGACRE	5/4/18		21. Ok. BTH. an offront to French DIV, - who to administrated by B.Q. XXII Corps Troops. Lead N.O. & forward to Corps for June. In Charge of Cartillon by Burn of Lt. News S.H.P. & 14/4/18 Who & gave Bains an order to attend y return Lt. DETERonin cleaned & returned only Store Wagon.	
"	16	7/4/18	Horn Stire & main dump to HUG? of every given. Calcubar un dump - To Stores delivered to Cluent - at Granger.	
GHYVELD (Brigerigh)	17/4/18		Bivouac dump cleared to Glenvorden. Only Stores before to no actually reported by units & Coy & returned a/ men an dump to main dump	

WAR DIARY or INTELLIGENCE SUMMARY

Army Form C. 2118.

Place	Date	Hour	Summary of Events and Information	Remarks and references to Appendices
G.H.Q. 2nd Echelon (Rouen)	18/4/18		Left Rouen to WATTEN (No 2 Gen. Hosp.) & collected 14 items	
			Same day. Visited Depts, Gen. Store & Ordnance with Staff Capt. & informed new Carrier Method of Indents during A.D.S.O. absence.	
			The difficulty appears to be in Departments not being in sufficiently close touch with Requisitioning Officers in regard to demands to be made.	
			In consequence of points having already been taken in view by D.A.D.O.S.	
"	24/4/18		Journey from Champs to Caal Huet via Calais to collect items Box Respirators — received returned Frame/Gauge mouthpieces etc — Dis & Hem Bags & Haversacks	
"	26/4/18		F.I.S. Sent to Base. Some difficulty appeared in returning state Returns to Imprest of various Railheads in Storage of their Reconsumption. Report this matter to A.D.O.S. 2nd Corps.	
"	30/4/18		Visit D.A.Q.L.M.G & 2nd Army to Acquet to collect 500 Small Box Respirators advised by COl. Atkins of A.D.M. S.H. Corps.	

M.W.Drama/Capt RAOC
21 Bn

May 1917.

Army Form C. 2118.

Dated 21 Aug.

WC 32

WAR DIARY
or
INTELLIGENCE SUMMARY.
(Erase heading not required.)

Place	Date	Hour	Summary of Events and Information	Remarks and references to Appendices
BOUVANCOURT	27/5	5 PM	Changes Army to FAVEROLLES et GOEMY	
FAVEROLLES	28/5	12 Noon	Changes group to ROMIGNY	
ROMIGNY	"	4.30 pm	Report received from DADMS 21 Div that Capt R.L. Quarrie had been wounded at POILLY and was being evacuated. One A/C RFC and 2 Rfgs	
			9 Kpfl.(attached) squadron wounded on returning from Railhead PROUILLY. One RFC (9 Roy(?)) arrived Kiosk at POILLY	
	29/5	9.0 pm	Changes Group to PASSY - GRIGNY + left with 21st MTC to K6, S.4 Sheet 22	
		5 pm	Report of Casualties sent to A.D.M.S. ASD IX Corp and S.C.8	
K6, S.4	30/5	10.15am	Stations horse of Capt R.S.QUARRIE A/SO opened in the presence of Lieut C.HENFREY ASC and Lieut and CROWTER A.C. Contents of kit+	
			Ropes over buspect money printed and verified with huf. + list + cash and effect sent to France 25 Cmts	
"	29/5	9.45 pm	16 lorries to 16 Vickers & H.G.B.P. 214 to Gun Park (21/4/18)	
	31/5	1.30 pm	Army moved to CHALTRAIT	
		11.20 pm	Proceeded with 2 lorries to O.O IX Corps Group and dress 40 Lewis Guns Comp. Returned at 3.35 A.m. 1/4/18 + reported to 21 Div 'Q'	

mf Brunner Capt A/C
L/O/S

June 1918.

WAR DIARY
or
INTELLIGENCE SUMMARY.
(Erase heading not required.)

Army Form C. 2118.

DADOS
21 Div.

Place	Date	Hour	Summary of Events and Information	Remarks and references to Appendices
CHALTRAIT	1/6/18	—	Wire received from ADOS IV Corps that Major G.M. DUCKWORTH had been ordered to report to Div. in relief of Capt. R. SQUARRIE.	
—	—	6-30 A.m.	Lt.Col. HOCKLEY proceeded to Divl. respective Brigades to collect materials from units in connection with "Rifle" vide our letter Q/1113 of 31/5/18	
—	—	11.45 A.m.	Visited Office of ADOS IX Corps. Demanded all Lewis & Vickers guns required to complete Divn. also 3" platoon film.	
—	—	9.40 P.m.	Wire recd. from Bde IX Corps that 2 Dvrs. & Stores were expected at Railhead	
EPERNAY	2/6/18	5-30 A.m.	Attended Railhead at midnight — 2 lorries attended with 2 lorries. Train not yet arrived.	
—	—		Received 12 Lewis Guns Comp. for 60th Rifle Brigade, arrangts made for 24 to be sent Lt/Col. Rifle Bde. to proceed to Railhead & report to ADOS IX Corps	
—	—		25 Kegs of Stores were dispatched to Lustry 1st — 3rd May 1918	
—	—		8 Units Lorries dispatched Railhead to clear & collect & Vickers guns. No trains arrived — lorries returned at 10 A.m. 2/6/18	
—	—	3.45 P.m.	Visited ADOS IX Corps & arranged to send 100 S.A.A. boxes to Divl. Gas School, arrd. to announce to dispatch 9 Lewis guns for 1st Corps vide QSA 1/653 of Div 16/5/18 —	

Army Form C. 2118.

WAR DIARY
or
INTELLIGENCE SUMMARY.
(Erase heading not required.)

DAQMS 21st Div

Place	Date	Hour	Summary of Events and Information	Remarks and references to Appendices
CHALTRAIT	3/16	Noon	Sent one lorry to O.O. of Corps troops for looking books + 3 lorries to EPERNAY Railhead to collect 2 trucks for 21st Div. also Coffee Trucks (manure + clean) (also late)	
		4pm	Collected & Picked game Comps. from O.O. IX Corps troops & delivered to 21st Gp. MG Coln by 10.30 p.m. at COURJEONNET. 2 truck not arrived.	
CONGY	4/16	6.30 am	Moved dump from CONTRAIT. Sent 3 lorries to COLLIGNY to look for the 2 trucks. Sent one lorry to CONTRAIT to collect 10th of reinforcements to distribute to units concerned. Tried Moreuin & Petit railhead to send salvage & surplus stores could be carried or dispatch to Base. R.T.O. could not accept.	
-	5/16	2.30 p.m.	Major G.M. Duckworth arrived for duty and assumed duty as DAQMG 21st Div. M.Sreevner Col	
-	5/18		Arrived for duty as DAQMS 21st Div. Reported to DHQ and DQMG IX Corps. Visited Morains le Petit & Vermontre to ascertain if salvage could be returned to Base. Cannot accept at present. Moved	
-	6/18		Dump into village of Congy, 10 Rue de Remy. Visited O.C. Corps troops to obtain horseshoes for Artillery. None available.	

Army Form C. 2118.

WAR DIARY
OF
INTELLIGENCE SUMMARY.
(Erase heading not required.)

Instructions regarding War Diaries and Intelligence Summaries are contained in F. S. Regs., Part II. and the Staff Manual respectively. Title pages will be prepared in manuscript.

Place	Date	Hour	Summary of Events and Information	Remarks and references to Appendices
CONGY	6/6/18		Called on ADOS II Corps re gun carriages &c. All guns spares and accessories to be dismantled thro' ADOS, also dies from Gun Park to be concentrated on central & distribution to be sent to Corps here	
"	7/6/18		Howitzer obtained from CC Concentration and sent to Artillery. Two trucks stores at Concentration Railhead. 6 sketches collected from Concentration for 65 Field Ambulance. Calles on ADOS and DDG. Lists sent from ADOS asking information re supply of gun &c.	
"	8/6/18		Called on Staff Capt RA to collect information re supplies. Lists to Sketches collected from Concentration and delivered to 64 Field Ambulance at Sezanne. Lists to Sketches	two lorry
			Loads of stores sent to Artillery and barrachée requirements completed.	
CONGY	9/6/18		Wire received from ADOS positioning experience. Moved stores from Congy to Les Bordes	
LES BORDES	10/6/18		Called on ADOS to arrange supply of stores. Two truck stores from Concentration	
"	11/6/18		Two trucks at Concentration brought up. CRA to be arranged re our billets. Two lorry loads of stores sent out to Artillery	
	12/6/18		Visited HQRS with regard to billets & general arrangements re food and water supplies etc.	
			Arranged for supply to be 20 et ml. from Park & now there	
			also for original	

WAR DIARY
or
INTELLIGENCE SUMMARY.

Army Form C. 2118.

A2005 21st Bn

Place	Date	Hour	Summary of Events and Information	Remarks and references to Appendices
LES BOVES	13/4/18		Letter on Staff Capt. to 63 Brigade re wheels for 151 Lincolns. Visited OC 151 Lincolns	
			Orders received to move to new area with the MT Coy at 515 am on 14th.	
"	14/4/18.		Left with MT Coy for new area. Spent night at Bernon	
Bernon	15/4/18		Continued journey and arrived night at Acoeure	
Martinsart	16/4/18		established dump and office at Martinsart	
			relieb and 1 general store returns from railhead	
"	17/4/18		Calls on S/TG, MGG. VII and HQ VIII Corps. Trove to from site for dump at Acheust. Nothing suitable at present. May be able to find accomodation on	
			above playground on Thursday	
"	18/6/18		Demanded 5000 Shirts and drawers from Army by order of HQ 2MG, Stop truck having already been demanded. Called on OO San Pool Way re Lorries	
			& Tons. Able to meet all our demands when submitted.	
"	19/6/18		Collected 2000 sets of items clothing from N° 1 Laundry at Allonville	
			Cleared store clothing and 1 truck relieb from railhead	
	20/6/18		Nothing of importance to report	
	21/6/18		Received orders to move to Garrache. 10 truck of clothing and general stores cleared from railhead. Visited Garrache in order to secure accomodation. Very difficult to find anything suitable.	

Army Form C. 2118.

WAR DIARY
or
INTELLIGENCE SUMMARY.
(Erase heading not required.)

Instructions regarding War Diaries and Intelligence Summaries are contained in F. S. Regs., Part II. and the Staff Manual respectively. Title pages will be prepared in manuscript.

Place	Date	Hour	Summary of Events and Information	Remarks and references to Appendices
Martinwells	22/6/18		March out 110 Brigade troops & officers from Martinwells to Samachio.	
Samachio	23/6/18		Served 63 Brigade troops to Samachio. Cleared truck vehicle and 3 truck of clothing equipment from railhead. Visited 1st Bn North Regt & 21st Batt S. Lancs and O.C.R.E. Arranged for two extra lorries for next three days, in order to run out all stores to the artillery. Demanded Lewis guns to complete all battalions to full strength.	
"	24/6/18		Visited 1st East Yorks, 15 Durhams L.I. and 9th KOYLI. Despatch 4 lorry teams of general stores to artillery. Collected French Mortars, Newton guns from Gun Park. Demanded 1 gun scarcity to complete artillery to full scale.	
"	25/6/18		Despatched 4 lorry teams to battery & shots & Pioneers. Collected Lewis guns to complete battalion to full strength for Gun Park. Visited O.C.R.E. and 9 KOYLI.	
"	26/6/18		8 Lewis to arrange for return of surplus reports equipment. All surplus equipment received from 9 KOYLI & Durhams. Unit instructed to show what is complete & establishment from 10th Advance Depot artillery. Visited O.C.R.E.	
"	27/6/18		Collected 9 - 6" Newton T.M. from Gun Park for distribution to y/51 & y/51 Batteries	
"	28/6/18		Orders received to re-equip the 9 KOYLI and Lewis guns for every stoneward on Gun Park	

Army Form C. 2118.

WAR DIARY
or
INTELLIGENCE SUMMARY.   Above H1.
(Erase heading not required.)

Place	Date	Hour	Summary of Events and Information	Remarks and references to Appendices
Gonnelin	29/6/18		Medical Artillery HQ, Headquarters 95" Brigade RFA ROC. 495 Battery billed out of 48. Four Guns received and same by G H 0421. Adv recce to Beyencourt move to new area.	
"	29/6/18		Demanded 1 Blyon Am How H.S. & limber am Wagon 4S How for 2 Sec DAC 1 limber How Wagon for 495 Btz and 1 limber 18 pr for 495 from 1 Am Col.	
"	30/6/18		Authority received to draw above and wish used to collect. Marched 10.00 31.8.02	

A6945 Wt. W14422/M160 350000 12/16 D. D. & L. Forms/C/2118/14

WAR DIARY
or
INTELLIGENCE SUMMARY

Army Form C. 2118.

(Erase heading not required.)

Instructions regarding War Diaries and Intelligence Summaries are contained in F. S. Regs., Part II. and the Staff Manual respectively. Title pages will be prepared in manuscript.

July 1918.

Vol 34

Place	Date	Hour	Summary of Events and Information	Remarks and references to Appendices
Karachi	1/7/18	8am	Received orders to meet arrival of barges	
Bungalow		4pm	Arrived at Sukkur Rd. Went off to supervise unloading of ammunition	
	2/7/18		United RDOS I Corps and ROO Road Survey made to unload OR to oversee	
			2 – 6" TMs to complete	
	3/7/18		Called on Gun Park no 3 to complete	
			OC D⁰⁶⁵ Field Ami turned clerk of station	
			to arrange for transport to be drawn from ordnance dept. Allahabad	
	4/7/18		Lorry sent out to Artillery Gun Park no 3 to	
	5/7/18		" " " "	
			Complete establishment of 24 + 4 MGs per battalion	
	6/7/18		Called on OC's I Coys, 1st, 2nd battns. 3 trick dhourie or rather	
	7/7/18		Lorry dispatched to Artillery Gun Park one brick chawer per rifle. 16 timer per rifle collected from Gun Park. 2 heavy guns received from B Batty 94 Bgde and	
			1 Vickers gun for machine gun Batt	
	8/7/18		Further three lorry loads dispatched to artillery. bogie roumt SM black	

Army Form C. 2118.

WAR DIARY
or
INTELLIGENCE SUMMARY.
(Erase heading not required.)

Instructions regarding War Diaries and Intelligence Summaries are contained in F. S. Regs., Part II. and the Staff Manual respectively. Title pages will be prepared in manuscript.

Place	Date	Hour	Summary of Events and Information	Remarks and references to Appendices
Bouquemaison	9/4/18		Collected from OC 9th Army Troops ammunition stores non for brigade. New guns for B Bty and Vickers gun for MG Bn received from Gun Park. One truck cleared from railhead.	
"	10/4/18		Called on AOOS V Corps and AVQ. Despatches 1 Lewis bush & plates to Artillery armament. 3 MG guns for AAC.	
"	11/4/18		Received visit of inspection from AOOS V Corps.	
"	12/4/18		Called on Gun Park to arrange for supply of rifle grenade dischargers & elliptical sights for AA guns. One truck general stores cleared from railhead.	
"	13/4/18		3 MG guns, 520 rifle grenade dischargers & 57 elliptical sights received from Gun Park and distributed. One truck clothing cleared from railhead. 3 lorry loads despatched to Artillery.	
"	14/4/18		1 truck general stores and 2 trucks vehicle stores from railhead. Collins and Swans. Used to 63 & 38 divisions.	
"	15/4/18		Attended conference at OZN on the care of ammunition at Refilling Point and the return of empties to railhead. Notices subsequent to give rate for next charges.	
"	16/4/18		Nothing of importance to report. One truck cleared from railhead. Orders to move cancelled. 18 pdrs ammunition for 139/5 RFA	

Army Form C. 2118.

WAR DIARY
or
INTELLIGENCE SUMMARY.
(Erase heading not required.)

Instructions regarding War Diaries and Intelligence Summaries are contained in F. S. Regs., Part II. and the Staff Manual respectively. Title pages will be prepared in manuscript.

Place	Date	Hour	Summary of Events and Information	Remarks and references to Appendices
Bouzincourt	17/4/18		Called O/H.Q. and 2/o/ M.G. Bn.. O.C. 2/M.G.Bn. reports that battalion is now fully equipped but requires further supplies of spare parts for vehicles. It was pointed out that it was very difficult to obtain at the moment and that at it recovery must be obtained in the war of some when supplies are received. Two lorry loads despatched to Artillery, also wagon annum 18pr & 18/95 R.F.A.	
"	18/4/18		Called on Staff Captain 63rd Brigade, O.C.s 15th Yorks, 9th K.O.Y.L.I. and 15th Durham L.I. All battalions report as fully equipped to scale.	
"	19/4/18		Called on 12/13 North'ns, 1 Lincolns, 2 Lincolns, all battalions complete. Called on 63rd Bde to arrange horsing arms. 63rd Bn do not wish to move their dumps from its present site. Demanded XXX complete Lewis guns to complete all battalions to scale G.	
"	20/4/18		Visited Rancheval to arrange site for next dump. Called on OO Army Troops 104 to arrange for supply of so clothing.	
"	21/4/18		Two lorry loads despatched to Artillery. One truck cleared at railhead. Sent for Lewis guns but could not extract them as they had not been released by Army.	

A6945 W₁ W₁₁₄₂₁/M₁₁₆₀ 350,000 12/16 D. D. & L. Forms/C./2118/14.

WAR DIARY
or
INTELLIGENCE SUMMARY.
(Erase heading not required.)

Army Form C. 2118.

Instructions regarding War Diaries and Intelligence Summaries are contained in F. S. Regs., Part II. and the Staff Manual respectively. Title pages will be prepared in manuscript.

Place	Date	Hour	Summary of Events and Information	Remarks and references to Appendices
Beaurains	22/7/18		92 Complete lewis gun collected from Lou Park. One truck cleared from railhead. Lewis dress clothing collected from XI Army Troops RE. 1500 containers for small box respirators demanded from Base to replace those in use over 40 hours. 16 Lewis gun demanded for A&MR.	
"	23/7/18		16 Lewis guns collected from Lou Park to complete all battns to to 46 per battn.	
"	24/7/18		One truck cleared from Railhead	
"	25/7/18		Moved office and dump from Beaurains to Rouchincourt.	
Rouchincourt	26/7/18		One truck cleared from Railhead. Visited 15 D.L.I. and M.G. Battn. N.C.O. to fix Clothing and O.R.P. Demanded 4.5 How to replace No 428 (condemned for wear.)	
do	27/7/18		Received reese from OOOS X Corps. Collected 4.5 How to replace no 428 and delivered same to 10M. Demanded 20000 S.A.A. blank cartridge	
do	28/7/18		Nothing to report.	
do	29/7/18		Visited Gas Batter, A.R.P. and S.A.O.S. 38 Bn re agricultural implements	
do	30/7/18		Proceeded on leave. 30/7/18 until 8/8/18	

Rouchincourt Maj n. D.A.D.O.S.

Army Form C. 2118.

WAR DIARY
or
INTELLIGENCE SUMMARY.
(Erase heading not required.)

Place	Date	Hour	Summary of Events and Information	Remarks and references to Appendices
Puchevillers	30.7.18	11 AM	Office visited by A.D.O.D. V Corps. 2 Trucks Cleared from Authuile. 3y trenches received for R.A. 200 drills DA sent to Siege Batts. ACHEUX via Vertal siding of Salieux. Sent to replace sent to Rouen (21 SDI).	
		3.15 PM	Authy. ordered by A.D.O.D. V Corps to collect from VII Corps RE Dump PUCHEVILLERS 150 Special Trench mortars - 30 to be delivered to Trench Dump LE QUESNOY and 120 to A.R.P. LEALVILLERS - ACHEUX road. 4 A.A. Portable mountings received from OC V Corps Troops 19 Anti Potable C.Is. (shells + tripods) received from OC V Corps troops.	
-do-	31.7.18	10 AM	Collected tools for opening packages from I Om 19/46 Omks Resurgence for use at A.R.P. Visited Div. Kingston Camp & 21st Divl. Coy. Conference with units. re: the return of G.S. in exchange for new issues.	
		11-15 AM	100 jackets or sent to Gen Batts + even despatched to O.C. V Corps Trs to collect 500 suits D.D. C.Is. to replace others effects with you.	

M Brenner
Lt Col
A D O C

WAR DIARY
INTELLIGENCE SUMMARY

Army Form C. 2118.

DADOS 21 Div

August 1917

Place	Date	Hour	Summary of Events and Information	Remarks and references to Appendices
Rainneval	1st		Two trucks cleared from Railhead	
		2 PM	Collected several repairing Elliptical MS sights from Nyob Omits. also 1 pr binoculars from 14 CLD Ones of the repair. Visited 21st SMT by re Clothing also OI Reception Camp & settled the question of a lorry repairer being attached to that camp permanently.	
do	2nd	9 AM	Delivered 16 Tools opening package to ARP at OBC 5.5 Short 57D. Also 220 yard Puttees to Gas bath ACHEUX. 5.2 Vickers .303" M.G. barrels received from Corps Pool for special operation. One truck cleared from Railhead	
do	3rd	10 AM	Visited Roo ROSEL re personnel disposal of old stores. 52 barrels Vickers MG delivered to MG Battn.	
do	4th		Delivered boots for Gum Boots to OO V Corp Troops. Visited Q.M. Stores 1st Bn J – no accumulation of stores found. Collected 17 rifles + 18 Imp Sulg helmets from Salvage Dump. AUCHEUX. Visited ARP at O 12 & 5.5 Short 57D and arranged to send Antigas labels Lunch. Visited Gas Battn & found disinfecting machinery out of order. Reported matter to AAA G	

WAR DIARY
or
INTELLIGENCE SUMMARY.
(Erase heading not required.)

Army Form C. 2118.

Place	Date	Hour	Summary of Events and Information	Remarks and references to Appendices
Rumebeval	5/12	9.20am	Div. HQ 'Q' phoned that 60 Torches Elec. + 150 Kashkarives were urgently required for special purpose. to be obtained from if possible. Kashkaries being made up in Ord. Depôt obte.	
		9.30am	Obtained Approval of ADOS V Corps of phone to purchase the Torches as time did not admit of obtaining these from the Base.	
		1.30pm	Obtained car & purchased 12 Torches at FLEXICOURT and 12	
do	6/12	3-30pm	at DOULLENS. Visited main Lorry dump at LEAVILLERS and ordered lorries would Expose the returnees to this dump. Proceeded to DOULLENS & purchased 18 Torches for issue to night.	
do	7/12	2.45pm	Office temp visited by ADOS Third Army & ADOS V CORPS	
do	8/12		Major Cholmondeley returned from leave and resumed duty McBrennen took over ADOS	
do	8/12		Received instructions from ADOS V Corps called on HQ V Corps + Returned DOC	

A6945 Wt. W11422/M1160 350,000 12/16 D.D. & L. Forms/C.2118/14.

WAR DIARY
or
INTELLIGENCE SUMMARY.

Army Form C. 2118.

Place	Date	Hour	Summary of Events and Information	Remarks and references to Appendices
Pancliceul	8/8/18		to discuss the subject of cleaning machines for harness, wheels &c.	
do	9/8/18		Dunnage BF 18 pdrs drawn from Gun Park for C/96 Bde RFA to replace damage by shell fire. 2 truck buggies + general stores drawn from railhead.	
			Called on Staff Captain RA re cleaning machines &c	
			Lewis Gun for 9 KYKI to replace one damaged by shell fire demanded from Gun Park.	
do	10/8/18		Lewis gun received from GP and issue to 9 KOYLI. Limber BF 18 pdr Carriage demanded for C/94 RFA to replace one damaged by shell fire.	
			Visited PRP to instruct AOC personnel with regard to packing of empties in accordance with OA/364/4 24/7/18 (OL/146 g 9/14)	
			Called on 21 M.G. Bn, SA 4 Section DAC, 97 Field Coy R.E, 12/13 North'n Bn, 1 Engr & 2 Lincoln Regt and M.2 Company Train and inspected OMs stores	
do	11/8/18		Accompanied RODS V Corps on visit of inspection to DAC and ARP	
			Called on Staff Captain Artillery to see if Horse Battery could left in the matter of packing empties before dispatch to ARP	
			Demanded O.Q.F. 18 pdrs for B/94 Bde to replace one condemned by IOM	
			One French bicycle + gener. stores cleared from railhead	

WAR DIARY
or
INTELLIGENCE SUMMARY.

(Erase heading not required.)

Army Form C. 2118.

Place	Date	Hour	Summary of Events and Information	Remarks and references to Appendices
Raincheval	12/8/18		Removed dumps and office to more suitable site.	
do	13/8/18		Called A.D.T.S. V Corps & proceeded to Doullens to purchase 12 Electric Torches. Visited Salvage dumps at Pinchurst & called on R.T.O. Puchevillers in search of services at Acheux Item.	
do	14/8/18		Collected O.B.E. 18/pr from M/px Bde from Gun Park and handed over 6100. Called on Brigade Transport Officers 64 T.O. and inspected transport 15 Yorks Regt, 9 KOYLI and 15 DLI and inspected gun stores. Collected 100 sets Pickmandles from O.I.C. T.M. and delivered to 2nd A.F. Bde and 10 sets to Machine Gun Batt."	
do	15/8/18		Called on O/3 Coy Brown, L.F. Wells Regt, 6th Bde & 7th Bn Leics Regt and inspected QMs stores. Issued 20 sets Packsaddles to 110 T.B. and 6 sets to 63rd Bde Ambulance.	
do	16/8/18		Collected famous cloth & fireplace etc from 14 & 18/47 Workshops for I Corps Agricultural Officer. 500 Sacks carrying water drawn from OO 3rd Army Corps Tps & Army L. Chalk and 250 delivered to Doctors 95 Bat 120 issued to 62 T.B.	

WAR DIARY
INTELLIGENCE SUMMARY

Army Form C. 2118.

Place	Date	Hour	Summary of Events and Information	Remarks and references to Appendices
Rainneville	16/8/18 (contd)		Visited ARP and taking of damage. Five truck gone alone closed for railway.	
"	17/8/18		Called on 64 Field Ambulance and inspected Gas store.	
"	18/8/18		Received clothing and equipment from general stores and from Rouen also called at ARP. Divisional Gas Posts & 4th Div. D.A.C.	
"	19/8/18		Called at ARP and Salvage dumps. Visited B/94 + C/94 Bdes R.F.A. and No 63 Field Ambulance and inspected 2 M.G. stores.	
			Demanded AA Lewis gun for B/95 Bde R.F.A. to replace one damaged by shell fire.	
"	24/8/18		Received 100 sets [?] from I Corps and issued 50 sets to 64 Brigade, 30 to 110 Brigade and 10 to Machine Gun Bn.	
"	25/8/18		The four Advance lorries were withdrawn at 1.30 am by orders of SMTO Y Corps. four DAQMG with regard to the matter and was told that for the present the Advance lorries were pooled and that demands for transport were to be submitted to him daily for the following day requirements.	
		4:30 AM	Lieut. 210814 advised as having been dispatched from Havre and	

WAR DIARY
or
INTELLIGENCE SUMMARY.

Army Form C. 2118.

(Erase heading not required.)

Place	Date	Hour	Summary of Events and Information	Remarks and references to Appendices
Raincheval	22/8/18		DAQMG asked for 3 lorries to clear stores from railhead. 8 sets pack saddles issued to 1.62 field Ambulance and 2 to Machine Gun Bn.	
	23/8/18		Railhead changed from Acheux to Vellu Eglise. Issued in 24 hours charges lorries did not report until 1 p.m. and instructions received from DAQMG that they could not be obtained.	
"			One truck general stores clear from railhead. Ordnance 18 pdr SF to replace an 18pdr recovered prisoner. Demanded for 5/Pos Fd RFA. also one damaged 2 2 inch light to replace lost. 500 magazines for Lewis guns received by order of DAQ May 300 assumed 6.62 Brigade.	
	24/8/18		Moved Office and dump to Acheux.	
"	25/8/18		Ammunition Park in situ & Acheux. Issued 1500 sacks each to 62, 64 & 110 Brigade. Issued 300 empty further to 110 Brigade.	
Mailly Maillet 9/9/18			Moved office and dump to Mailly Maillet. Demands further 500 Magazines and issued 200 to 64 Brigade, 100 to 62 Brigade and 200 to SAA Section. Demanded further 3600 pro socks from Ordnance Park for stock. Collected 500	

WAR DIARY or INTELLIGENCE SUMMARY

Army Form C. 2118.

Place	Date	Hour	Summary of Events and Information	Remarks and references to Appendices
Mailly Maillet	27/9/18		Issued 600 pm sacks each to 62, 63, 64 & 110 Brigades. Demanded GF 18 per unit BM for C/94 Bde RFA to replace no lost reinforcement for convoy.	
do	28/9/18		Collected 18 pdr gun & carriage for C/94 Bde RFA. One long load of stores serviceable stores collected from Beaumont and one lay lost when delivered to Artillery units. Wired to DOS V Corps for 30 Yukon packs urgently required by 110 Brigade. Collected same from 2nd Army Troops Dizie le Chateau and delivered to Hd Qrs Bde. 50 French Shells collected from CC Cap Hqrs of 14th Div 6th Bde.	
do	29/9/18		Collected further 15 French Shells from OC Cap Korps and delivered to Hd Qrs of 6 Hd Qs 6th Bde. Demanded 19 Lewis Guns for 2 RSLI to replace same rendered damaged by shell fire. Submitted one day load of stores to Artillery to arrive 300 Zeller consisting of each Brigade. Carriers Cart etc and 50 per Blankette to DSC Inspected 100 fur coats, 5 galls dub'c & vic, and 500er fluvellette to Staff	
do	30/9/18		Captains of each Brigade. 5 galls received old to Staff Captain Artillery Demanded further quantity flannelette and oil lubricating for sniper Inspected Lary to 00 3rd Army Korps No 2 Battalion to collect 1500 water bottle. Above clearances changed & despatch para return.	

Army Form C. 2118.

WAR DIARY
or
INTELLIGENCE SUMMARY.
(Erase heading not required.)

Instructions regarding War Diaries and Intelligence Summaries are contained in F. S. Regs., Part II. and the Staff Manual respectively. Title pages will be prepared in manuscript.

Place	Date	Hour	Summary of Events and Information	Remarks and references to Appendices
Mailly Maillet	2/9/18		Demanded 5 Lewis Guns for 1 Lincoln Regt. to replace some number damaged by shell fire and collected same from Ord Park Burchworth D.A.D.O.S. 2/st Div	

WAR DIARY
or
INTELLIGENCE SUMMARY.
(Erase heading not required.)

Army Form C. 2118.

Instructions regarding War Diaries and Intelligence Summaries are contained in F. S. Regs., Part II. and the Staff Manual respectively. Title pages will be prepared in manuscript.

Place	Date	Hour	Summary of Events and Information	Remarks and references to Appendices
Mailly Maillet	2/9/18		Demanded 5 Lewis Guns for 1 Lincoln Regt. to replace same under damage by shell fire and collected same from Gun Park Hedauville. Drops 2nd O.R.	

Army Form C. 2118.

WAR DIARY
or
INTELLIGENCE SUMMARY.
(Erase heading not required.)

Place	Date	Hour	Summary of Events and Information	Remarks and references to Appendices
Mailly Maillet	27/9/18		Issued 600 p.a.a. sacks each to 62, 64 & 110 Brigades. Demanded 8 F 18 pr. amn. BM for C/94 Bde RFA to replace 657 condemned for firing.	
do	28/9/18		Collected 18 robs guns & carriages for C/94 Bde RFA. One lorry load of salvage serviceable stores collected from Beaumont and one lorry load also delivered to Artillery units. Wired to ADOS V Corps for 30 Yukon packs urgently required by 110 Brigade. Collected arms from C/B 2nd Army Troops. Issue to Chateau and delivered to Hd Qrs Bde. 50 Stouke shells collected from OB Coye Depot & Hd Qrs 64 Bde.	
do	29/9/18		Collected further 15" trench Mortar from O.O.C. Troops and delivered to Hd Qrs of C/62 Bde 64 Bde Btn. Demanded 19 Lewis Guns for C.R.A. VII to replace condemned. Demanded by shell firing. Authorised one lorry load of stone to Artillery to and 200 mile sandbags to each Brigade. 5 galls lub. oil and 5 galls flannelette to Staff Captain Artillery Despatched 700 fur socks, 5 galls lub. oil and 5 gals flannelette to Staff Captain Artillery	
do	30/9/18		Captains of each Brigade. 5 galls mineral oil to Staff Captain Artillery. Demanded further quantity flannelette and oil, lubricating, over. Despatched party 5.00 2nd Army Troops No 2 Auxiliary to collect 3500 old blankets. Moved divisional dumps & dispatched pers. return.	

A6945 W¹ W11142/M1160 350,000 12/16 D.D.&L. Forms/C/2118/14.

Army Form C. 2118.

BAOS 21st Div

WAR DIARY
or
INTELLIGENCE SUMMARY.
(Erase heading not required.)

September 1918.

VOL 36

Place	Date	Hour	Summary of Events and Information	Remarks and references to Appendices
Mailly Maillet	1/9/18		Called at DHQ. Despatched 1 lorry load stores including 19 furniture for QROWN.	
			5 ft. 1 Lincoln suit 8 for 12/13 NF. Also 1 lorry load clothing for various units.	
			Supply railhead changed from Beauval to Aubigny.	
			Railhead but nothing to collect.	
do	2/9/18		Called at DHQ. 1/9 KOYLI, 15 DLI and 12 Yorks Regt. Despatched 450 pairs socks to each infantry brigade, also 1 horse gauge wagon to various units and collected 2 loads of salvage ironmongery to store for re-issue.	
			Standard complete lament Cols Butler for 1st Bn Wiltshire Regt.	
			Called at new railhead to arrange return of serviceable stores & any clothing called on DADS.	
do	3/9/18		Our lorry had special stores duplicate to various units also one load of clothing to 64 Fd amb. and one line to Artillery.	
			Our truck served stores cleared from railhead and one lorry load of clothing and 6 railheads for despatch to No. 1 Ord. Laundry Arbuthill.	
			Despatched 19 store lures for 15 A.F.A. & for KOYLI, to 12 Yorks Regt and uniforms for 15 A.F.A., also Ordnance QF 18 pdr for 19/4 R.F.A. and 2-3 Stokes Mortar	

WAR DIARY or INTELLIGENCE SUMMARY.

Army Form C. 2118.

Place	Date	Hour	Summary of Events and Information	Remarks and references to Appendices
Hedlly Hurtel	3/9/18		for 110 Trench Mortar Battery	
do	4/9/18	10.30am	Despatch lorry to Gun Park to exchange the 12 Lewis Guns for the 69 Infantry Brigade and Trench Mortar	
do			Called at B.H.Q. and 10th and 11th Lincoln Regt. Visited Beaulencourt to arrange for removal of Stores and dump. Despatched 1 back store to Bart. Battery, 6th & 110 Brigades, also Lewis guns on demand for 9th N.O.Y.L.I. 15th D.L.I. and 15th York Regt. Transmitted 20 Lewis guns for 15th York Regt. 10 for y Lincoln Regt.	
Beaulencourt	5/9/18		Moved office and dump to Beaulencourt. Railhead changed to Beaulencourt and one clothing and one trench journal store. Delivered 20 Lewis guns to 1 E York Regt. and 10 to 7 Durants Inft.	
do	6/9/18		Work commences up to Beaulencourt Despatches one bury trail store to 62 Brigade	
do	7/9/18		Called at B.H.Q. Despatched one bury back stores to 110 Infantry Brigade and one to R.D.C. Machine Gun Bn. and various other units. Received vivit from A.D.O.S. Corps.	
do	8/9/18		Despatched 1 bury back stores to 62 & 110 Infantry Brigades. Elence 3 lorry	

WAR DIARY
or
INTELLIGENCE SUMMARY.

(Erase heading not required.)

Army Form C. 2118.

Instructions regarding War Diaries and Intelligence Summaries are contained in F. S. Regs., Part II. and the Staff Manual respectively. Title pages will be prepared in manuscript.

Place	Date	Hour	Summary of Events and Information	Remarks and references to Appendices
Boulenwood	8/9/18		Coeds captured Trench Mortars from Petit-Miramont Salvage dump.	
			Collected 14 supplies Bren Gun from 1st Yorks Regt. and issued 6 to 6th Leinster Regt. and 8 to Divis 38th Division. Cleared one lorry load Bren Books from old dump at Mailly Maillet.	
do	9/9/18		Pulled out 1st Yorks Regt., 9 KOYLI, 15 DLI and 12th + 2nd Lincolns Regt.	
			Dispatched 1 lorry load of stores to 62 & 64 TMB. and 1 lorry load to Divl. Artillery. One lorry load clean underclothing delivered to Staff Capt. 62 Brigade.	
			Forwarded 2 water cart, 2 Wagons limbers and 3 Kitchens limbers for 9th KOYLI to replace new arrivals destroyed by shell fire.	
			Forwarded 1 Wagon limbered for 1st Yorks Regt. to replace one destroyed by shell fire.	
do	10/9/18		Called on Mr Templeton Camp to arrange supply of SD Clothing. One truck general stores cleared from Railhead. 1 Lorry load cloths delivered to 62, 64, 110 Brigades. 1000 pairs socks collected from 17 Divl. Batts Rocquigny and SD Pierro per Battalion delivered to	

Army Form C. 2118.

WAR DIARY
or
INTELLIGENCE SUMMARY.
(Erase heading not required.)

Instructions regarding War Diaries and Intelligence Summaries are contained in F. S. Regs., Part II. and the Staff Manual respectively. Title pages will be prepared in manuscript.

Place	Date	Hour	Summary of Events and Information	Remarks and references to Appendices
Beaulencourt	9/9/18		64 Infantry Brigade. Two lorry load stores collected from Bially Mailet and three loads from Salvage dumps and sent to rear dumps.	
do	10/9/18		Called on O.O. Advanced Gun Parks to arrange for return of 6" Mortar TMB's. Despatched one lorry load stores to 64 Brigade and one load to 110 Brigade. 1500 pm socks delivered to 110 Brigade (500 per battalion). 3 Napoleon Lewis Guns issued to 2 Lincoln Regt to replace lost. 11 Steinmeyers sent to Base.	
do	12/9/18		One lorry load stores delivered to Corpl Artillery and one load to 63 Infantry Brigade. Packs of 14th N.F. (Pioneers) collected from near dump at Le Bar and delivered to unit. Transport lines to Pick Gun Wheel for Artillery collected from 62 & 64 BdsA	
do	9/9/18		South W.A. Brennan returned from one month's engagement leave in United Kingdom. Two trucks, one of clothing and one of Boundary, cleared from railhead. 1500 pairs socks delivered to Staff Captain 64th Brigade. One lorry load stores delivered to 62 & 64 & 110 Brigade. 2 Lewis guns to replace lost rifles destroyed by shell fire issued to 1 Bn Lincoln Regt. 32 Hooges machine and 32 Hooges Rifled slings collected from 16 Corps Range and delivered to Machine Gun School.	

A9045 (Wt. W1742/M160 350,000 12/16 D.D. & L. Forms/C/2118/14.

Army Form C. 2118.

WAR DIARY
or
INTELLIGENCE SUMMARY.
(Erase heading not required.)

Instructions regarding War Diaries and Intelligence
Summaries are contained in F. S. Regs., Part II.
and the Staff Manual respectively. Title pages
will be prepared in manuscript.

Place	Date	Hour	Summary of Events and Information	Remarks and references to Appendices
Beaulincourt	14/9/18		Demanded 2 Lewis Guns for 1 WELR Regt case 16 for 12/13 North Robs, collected same from Gun Park and delivered to units.	
			3 Lorry loads of stores despatched to Div Artillery, 62 & 110 Brigades. Called at Div H.Q. Proceeded to Doullens and purchased 33 Clothes brushes required for special purpose and delivere same to the 62 Brigade.	
do	15/9/18		Demanded 18 pdr QF for 1195 RFA to replace no 6981 condemned for wear. Demanded 13 Lewis guns for 15 Pdr OR1 and delivered same to unit. 4 Vickers guns demanded for 21 Div. M G Coy, and 3 Lewis guns for 15 Yorks Regt. Our truck gained stores eleven four rattles and one Lewis gun stores delivered to Infantry Brigades.	
do	16/9/18		Called O.N.Q, Staff Captain 110 Brigade, 6th Leicester, 7th Leicester, 1 Wilts, 1st Lincoln, 2nd Lincoln Regt and SMA Gorton O.R.C. One Lorry Load stores despatched to Div. Artillery and 2 Loads to 62, 110 & 64 Brigade. Collected 3 Vickers guns for 21 MG Coy and 3 Lewis guns for 15 Yorks Regt from Gun Park. 200 magazine for Lewis Guns taken from dump of 9 KOYLI and delivered to Div Ammun. Dump. Maricourt and the number demanded from Gun Park to replace.	

WAR DIARY
or
INTELLIGENCE SUMMARY.

Army Form C. 2118.

Place	Date	Hour	Summary of Events and Information	Remarks and references to Appendices
Beaulencourt	17/9/18		Proceeded to Doullens by rail & C.U.P.H.Q and purchased 10 metres yellow cloth for the manufacture of small flags. 110 flag-mats are delivered to D.H.Q. Further 190 magazines for Lewis guns delivered to Divisional Supply Refilment. One truck clothing chits from railhead. 4 Vickers guns delivered to 21 Machine Gun Battn. and 3 Lewis guns to 1 F Yorks Regt.	
do	18/9/18		One lorry with cloths dispatched to 62 & 110 Infantry Brigades and one load to hut artillery	
do	19/9/18		One truck general stores chits from railhead and one lorry load stores dispatched to 62 B.I.Brigade. 1200 pairs socks arrive to each respectively Brigade and same number to refill demands by wire from Base. Two Vickers guns for 21 Machine Gun Bn. to refill some damages to rifles from demand from Gun Park.	
do	20/9/18		Moved dumps to Rocquigny. One lorry load of cloths dispatched to artillery units and one load to units of 110 Brigade.	
Rocquigny	21/9/18		Moved office to Rocquigny. Billets at D.H.Q. Issued one truck clothing from railhead. Demanded 4 Lewis Guns for 1 st Wilts Regt. to refill same number lost destroyed by shellfire. Also one no food supply for our Reception Camp.	
do	22/9/18		One lorry load stores dispatched to artillery. Rifles etc. and machine gun batt.	

Army Form C. 2118.

WAR DIARY
or
INTELLIGENCE SUMMARY.
(Erase heading not required.)

Instructions regarding War Diaries and Intelligence Summaries are contained in F. S. Regs., Part II. and the Staff Manual respectively. Title pages will be prepared in manuscript.

Place	Date	Hour	Summary of Events and Information	Remarks and references to Appendices
Rocquigny	23/9/18		Cleared 3 trucks (9500) blankets, 1 truck general store & 1 truck laundry from railhead. Called O.N.O. and 10 pm 19/us Ordnance Workshops. Issued 3 above Lewis guns to 1st Bn Lincoln Regt.	
do	24/9/18		9000 Leather jerkins collected from OC V Corps troops and issues made to all infantry and machine gun battalions. 2 Lewis guns demanded for 15th Bn D.L.I. and 3 A.S.P. Lewis gun demanded for 21 Kingston Compy. Transferred Hd Qrs A,B,C and B5, 95 RFA Bde and No 2 Sec O.M.C. to OC VI Corps Troops.	
do	25/9/18		Issued 30 sets Packsaddlery to each Infantry Brigade. Ordnance Q.F. H.S Hour. demanded for 15/94 R.F.A. to replace in 400 condemned for wear.	
do	26/9/18		Cleared one truck general stores from railhead. Collected 100 sacks carrying underlin from OC 3rd Army Lwgh. No 2 and issued 30 to each infantry brigade.	
do	27/9/18		Cleared one truck general stores and blanket from railhead. Issued 200 Lewis gun magazines to Bn Ammn Dumps and 200 to 64 Infantry Brigade. Cancelled mem of 95 RFA Bde. by order of Staff Captain R.A.	
do	28/9/18		Cleared one truck clothing from railhead. Deficiencies are very bad.	

WAR DIARY
or
INTELLIGENCE SUMMARY.

Army Form C. 2118.

Place	Date	Hour	Summary of Events and Information	Remarks and references to Appendices
Rocquigny	28/9/18		to Artillery. Demanded 2 Vickers guns for 21 MG Bn and range our retrepeals with sight for C/95 RFA to replace those damaged by shell fire.	
do	29/9/18		Carry back stores despatched to 95 Brigade RFA	
do	30/9/18		Railhead changed from Rocquigny to Ims. Lorries with stores despatched to each infantry brigade and D.C. Artillery. Demanded Lewis gun complete for 1st East Yorkshire Regt.	

Murchunt Major
DADOS 21st Div.

No 37

CONFIDENTIAL.

WAR DIARY

D.A.D.O.S., 21st Division.

October 1st - 31st 1918.

WAR DIARY
or
INTELLIGENCE SUMMARY
(Erase heading not required)

DADOS 21st Div. Army Form C. 2118.
October 1918

Place	Date	Hour	Summary of Events and Information	Remarks and references to Appendices
FINS	1/10/18		Moved office and dump from ROCQUIGNY to FINS. Delivered 1500 pairs socks to each infantry Brigade. Demanded Lewis Gun for 2 Bn Lincoln Regt. to replace one damaged by shell fire.	
do	2/10/18		Called on 1 Bn Lincoln Regt, 2 Bn Queens Regt and D/3 Bn Northumberland Fusiliers. Visited Gas Baths Equancourt to arrange for return of S.D. Clothing left there by 17th Division. Demanded complete equipment 4.5 How. for 9/9 L R.F.A. to replace Gun No 1942 and carriage No 84894 destroyed by premature. One truck vehicle stores from railhead.	
do	3/10/18		Received visit from ADOS V Corps.	
do	4/10/18		Called on 1 Bn Wilts Regt, 6th Bn Lincoln Regt, 9th Bn Lincoln Regt, 9th Bn K.O.Y.L.I., 15th Bn Durham L.I. and 1st Bn E York Regt and 34th Bn Labour O.T.C. Issued 600 pro coats to Divisional Baths.	
do	5/10/18		Demanded 2 complete Lewis guns for 6th Lincoln Regt to replace others lost. Issued 3 salved infantry Lewis guns to 2 Lincoln Regt to replace lost. One truck clothing & stores from railhead.	

Army Form C. 2118.

WAR DIARY
or
INTELLIGENCE SUMMARY.

(Erase heading not required.)

Instructions regarding War Diaries and Intelligence Summaries are contained in F. S. Regs., Part II. and the Staff Manual respectively. Title pages will be prepared in manuscript.

Place	Date	Hour	Summary of Events and Information	Remarks and references to Appendices
FINS	6/10/18		Called on No 1 & 3rd Companies. Dull rain. Cleared one truck general stores from railhead. Demanded 4 Lewis guns for 1 Lincoln Regt, also carriage 18 pdr for C/94 Bde RFA to replace no 99368.	
do	7/10/18		Called 51 HQ and 64 Field Ambulance.	
do	8/10/18		One lorry load stores delivered to 2' Devt Artillery and one load to 110 Inf Bde.	
do	9/10/18		One lorry load of plates delivered to 62 & 64 Infantry Brigades. Called at 51 HQ.	
do	10/10/18		Despatched 2 lorry loads Blankets to brigades to complete infantry battalions to scale of 1 blanket per man. Demanded carriage 4.5 how with carrier disc eighteen I for D/95 Bde RFA to replace no 62009 destroyed by shell fire.	
do	11/10/18		Moved office and pant of dump to WALINCOURT. Cleared one truck of general stores from railhead. Demanded 2 corp. Lewis guns for 2nd Bn Lincoln Regt.	
WALINCOURT				
do	12/10/18		Continued on work of clearing dump from FINS. Demanded one 3" Stokes T.M. complete for 110 TM Bty.	
do	13/10/18		Completed clearance of dump at Fins. Demanded 2 complete Lewis guns for	

A6945 Wt. W11422/M1160 336,000 12/16 D. D. & L. Forms/C/2118/14.

Army Form C. 2118.

WAR DIARY
or
INTELLIGENCE SUMMARY.
(Erase heading not required.)

Place	Date	Hour	Summary of Events and Information	Remarks and references to Appendices
HAVRINCOURT	13/10/18	contd.	1st East Yorks. Regt and 2 for 13th Bn Durham L.I.	
			Called on 51st Bn Machine Gun Corps and inspected 2 Mn stores and arranged for with OC to ask for an armourer & Cpl. to complete establishment	
do	14/10/18		Cleared our truck clothing and 2 Lew Lewis Lempling from Base issued 7 Lewis guns from local resources to 4th Bn Lincolns Regt.	
			Demanded 3 complete Lewis guns for 12/13 Bn D.L.I., one 18 pdr gun for A/94 Bde RFA to replace no 3310 condemned for inaccuracy, also 4.5" How: on 13 M.B. for D/95 Bde RFA to replace No 1427 destroyed by shell fire.	
do	15/10/18		Railhead changed to MASNIERES. Called on ADOST Corps and units, new railhead to arrange for return of old state.	
do	16/10/18		One truck of general stores cleared from railhead. Horse clipping machine received from Base	
do	17/10/18		Issued one Lewis gun to 6 yr Lincolns Regt.	
do	18/10/18		Called on ADOST Corps with reference regarding supply of winter clothing. Demanded 2 complete Lewis guns for 1st Bn Wiltshire Regt to replace lost.	

A0945 Wt. W11422/M1160 359000 12/16 D. D. & L. Forms/C/2118/4.

WAR DIARY or INTELLIGENCE SUMMARY

Army Form C. 2118.

Place	Date	Hour	Summary of Events and Information	Remarks and references to Appendices
MALINCOURT	19/10/18		Demanded one limber Q.F. 18 pdr wagon for C/94 Bde R.F.A. to replace one condemned, also reserve QF. 18 pdrs for B/95 Bde R.F.A. to replace no 11166 condemned for carry. Sent Draper A.V.D. inspector of boot repairing shops, arrived for duty from 3005 II Corps. Visited CAUDRY.	
do	20/10/18		Sent Draper inspector divisional boot & shoe shops of the 62nd Infantry Brigade.	
do	21/10/18		Demanded 18 pdr gun & carriage to replace numbers 1904 and 4755 for C/95 Bde. R.F.A. One truck horseless vehicle cleared from railhead. Sent Draper inspector bootshops of 110 Infantry Bde.	
do	22/10/18		Demanded 18 pdr with Br. for C/94 Brigade R.F.A. to replace no 3284.	
INCHY	23/10/18		Moved office and dump from MALINCOURT to INCHY. 12 lorries arrived general store from railhead, lorry at 10 pm to Guiscard to collect 12 complete lewis guns urgently required by 1 Bn 4 Wilts Regt.	
do	24/10/18		Slaughtered 12 lewis guns to 1st WWR Regt. Also 1500 pr. each to each 2 pdrs. Brower	

WAR DIARY
or
INTELLIGENCE SUMMARY.
(Erase heading not required.)

Army Form C. 2118.

Place	Date	Hour	Summary of Events and Information	Remarks and references to Appendices
INCHY	24/10/18		Delivered one lorry load general stores and a supply of rifle oil to units of 64th Infantry Brigade. Demanded 18 pdr guns for B/95 Bde R.F.A. to replace no 5 ordinance by 10 M for evening. Stores are back again also from railhead.	
do	25/10/18		Three loads of white clothing drawn from railhead. Visited railhead and old dump at REMINCOURT.	
do	26/10/18		Visited railheads and D.T.Q. to arrange for supply of ammunition for troops coming out of the line. Called on 1st Lincoln Regt. and 21st Bn Machine Gun Corps.	
do	27/10/18		Called at D.H.Q. and visited Q.M. Sergeants of NEUVILLY. Obtained return ammunition of all infantry supplies and buried load of general stores to 10th Brigade at EUVRES.	
do	28/10/18		Called on Lord D [illegible] returning to railhead supply. Visited railway and called on A.D.O.S. V Corps. Secured 10 Lewis guns to 1st East Yorks Regt and 16 to 15th Bn Durham L.I. from local resources 13 being obtained from Orders 17th Division.	

WAR DIARY
or
INTELLIGENCE SUMMARY.
(Erase heading not required.)

Army Form C. 2118.

Place	Date	Hour	Summary of Events and Information	Remarks and references to Appendices
INCHY	26/10/18		Demanded 6 complete Lewis guns for 9/13 Bn Northumberland Fusiliers and 12 guns only for 9th Bn KOYLI, also 9 complete guns for 6th Bn Lincolns Regt. Wired for our Kitchen travelling boxes for 12th & 13th Fld Ryt. Sent a supply of service dress clothing and clean underclothing to Divisional Reception Camp. Were received from ADOS I Corps that trucks meant to be cleared immediately on arrival of empty train. Sent a runner to railhead who remained all night but the train did not arrive. Called on RTO Cantley and arranged that a runner should be sent to this office to announce the arrival of the train. Wired for 3 Vickers guns for the 2nd Bn. Machine Gun Corps and three 3" Stokes mortars for the 6th TM Cy.	
do	29/10/18		Collected two boxes of dirty underclothing from 62nd & 116th Inf Brigades and one load of repairable Lewis guns mag magazines, captured German gear etc from Salvage dump.	
do	30/10/18		Cleared three truck worth service clothing, one truck coverings, one truck laundry	

A6945 Wt. W1422/M1160 350,000 12/16 D. D. & L. Forms/C./2118/14

Army Form C. 2118.

WAR DIARY
or
INTELLIGENCE SUMMARY.
(Erase heading not required.)

Place	Date	Hour	Summary of Events and Information	Remarks and references to Appendices
INCHY	30/10/18		One truck which and one of general stores from northern CAUDRY.	
			Delivered by lorry 16 Livres guns to 15th Bde O.L.S. 12 to 9th Bn KOYLI	
			and 6 to 12/13 Bn Northumberland Fus.	
INCHY	31/10/18		Despatched 3 lorry loads stores to 62, 64 & 110 Infantry Brigades	
			Billet as southwest.	
			Successfully Major RAOC	

Army Form C. 2118.

WAR DIARY
or
INTELLIGENCE SUMMARY.
(Erase heading not required.)

Instructions regarding War Diaries and Intelligence Summaries are contained in F. S. Regs., Part II. and the Staff Manual respectively. Title pages will be prepared in manuscript.

DADS 31st Division

November 1918

WO 38

Place	Date	Hour	Summary of Events and Information	Remarks and references to Appendices
INCHY	1/11/18.		Delivered 1500 p.s sacks from laundry to each infantry brigade, also one lorry load general stores to each brigade. Called at salvage dump and arranged for exchange of captured German machine guns, serviceable Lewis gun magazines, Signal pistol &c.	
do	2/11/18.		Leave one lorry clothing from railhead. Sent a supply of Lewis gun magazines by lorry to 9th Bn KOYLI.	
do	3/11/18.		Called at DHQ and arranged for a lorry containing sacks, flannelette, rifle oil, magazines for Lewis guns to be attached to HQ during the advance. Visited railhead and found that it was likely to change for the next few days owing to destruction caused by mines. One truck gunnin store cleared.	
do	4/11/18.		Despatched lorry containing 5000 p.s sacks, 10 galls rifle oil, 5 galls buffer oil, 1000 yds flannelette, 400 magazines to Lewis guns to DHQ as arranged. Railhead changed to CAMBRAI. Visited railhead and cleared one truck whole gunnin one truck gunnin stores.	
do	5/11/18.		Three lorry loads of dirty underclothing and unserviceable ordnance sent to railhead. Great difficulty experienced on disposing of the stores, the lorries being away for 12 hours.	

Army Form C. 2118.

WAR DIARY
or
INTELLIGENCE SUMMARY.
(Erase heading not required.)

Instructions regarding War Diaries and Intelligence Summaries are contained in F. S. Regs., Part II. and the Staff Manual respectively. Title pages will be prepared in manuscript.

Place	Date	Hour	Summary of Events and Information	Remarks and references to Appendices
INCHY	6/11/18		One lorry with general stores despatched to 110 Inf Brigade, also one 6 cwt Inf Brigade which failed to return.	
do	7/11/18		One lorry with stores for Divl Artillery despatched and failed to return.	
do	8/11/18		Lorry returned from 6 cwt Inf Bde having been delayed owing to the bad state of the roads. 3000 sets clean underclothing sent to Div HQ at Berlaimont for distribution.	
BERLAIMONT	9/11/18		Moved Office and dump to BERLAIMONT. Artillery lorry returned.	
do	10/11/18		Draw one 12/13th Bn Northumberland Fus., 1st Lincoln Rgt & 1st Lincoln Rgt.	
do	11/11/18		Demanded 3000 sets of Service dress clothing by wire from Base by orders of G.O.C. Cleared out used clothing from railhead CAVDRY.	
do	13/11/18		Called on Staff Captain 110 Bde., 1st Bn Lincolnshire Regt and 1st Bn Wiltshire regt.	
do	16/11/18		Wired to Base for supply of blankets for personnel vehicles of divisions. Despatched one load of extras to Morley mill.	
do	17/11/18		Demanded wagon issue of BF 18/Pdr and howr wagons ammn Repair for C Bty 95 Bde RFA to refill also ammunition by 10A.M.	

A6945 Wt. W14422/M1160 350,000 12/16 D. D. & L. Forms/C./2118/14.

Army Form C. 2118.

WAR DIARY
or
INTELLIGENCE SUMMARY.
(Erase heading not required.)

Instructions regarding War Diaries and Intelligence Summaries are contained in F. S. Regs., Part II. and the Staff Manual respectively. Title pages will be prepared in manuscript.

Place	Date	Hour	Summary of Events and Information	Remarks, and references to Appendices
BERLAIMONT	18/11/18		Railhead changed to SOLESMES.	
do	19/11/18		Called at railhead and arranged to start a dump near by. This was necessary owing to the large number of trucks retained as having been defaulted from base, and the impossibility of clearing them to BERLAIMONT with available transport.	
do	20/11/18		Three Brigade Warrant Officers, two rank & file clerks and one storeman enlisted hospital with influenza. Position reported to DOES S.S. Army and ROOT.D Corps by wire and reinforcements asked for. Two trucks general stores, one truck clothing and one truck laundry cleared from railhead and dumped at SOLESMES.	
do	21/11/18		Visited railhead SOLESMES and cleared two lorry loads of clothing to dump at BERLAIMONT. Q asked for 6 additional lorries to help move the remainder of the stores from SOLESMES	
do	22/11/18		Cleared 4 trucks Blankets and dumped at SOLESMES. Seven lorry loads general stores removed from SOLESMES to BERLAIMONT	

Army Form C. 2118.

WAR DIARY
or
INTELLIGENCE SUMMARY.
(Erase heading not required.)

Instructions regarding War Diaries and Intelligence Summaries are contained in F.S. Regs., Part II. and the Staff Manual respectively. Title pages will be prepared in manuscript.

Place	Date	Hour	Summary of Events and Information	Remarks and references to Appendices
BERLAIMONT	22/11/18		One sergeant (clerk) and one storeman arrived for temporary duty in place of men evacuated to H.	
do	23/11/18		Called at railhead SOLESMES. A Branch asked for additional transport to clear Blankets and deliver same to units.	
do	24/11/18		Collected one lorry loads of Blankets from SOLESMES and delivered same to units.	
do	25/11/18		Cleared two further loads of Blankets from SOLESMES and supplied to lorry loads general store to Corps artillery. Reserve of box respirators returned to Base by valise of DADMG.	
do	26/11/18		Railhead moved to SALESMES.	
do	27/11/18		Called at new railhead and arranged to open a dump ready for the receipt of ammunition etc. One lorry was again deputed to move artillery.	
do	28/11/18		Urgent machine sent to Base for laundry and pay Book. Instructions received from ADOS and to return any slow serviceable forth machineSaw	

A6945 Wt. W14422/M1160 350,000 12/16 D.D. & L. Forms/C/2118/14

Army Form C. 2118.

WAR DIARY
or
INTELLIGENCE SUMMARY.
(Erase heading not required.)

Instructions regarding War Diaries and Intelligence Summaries are contained in F. S. Regs., Part II. and the Staff Manual respectively. Title pages will be prepared in manuscript.

Place	Date	Hour	Summary of Events and Information	Remarks and references to Appendices
BERLAIMONT	29/10/18		Called at Railhead.	
			ADMS V Corps called for report on supply of boot ankles. Position reported by wire.	
do	30/10/18		Called at Railhead and at Nos 3, 19 & 21 CCSs Enquiry to obtain particulars of WOs and men evacuated with influenza. Found that all had been evacuated to Base. Reinforcements demanded.	

J. Mouchwards Major

Vol 39

CONFIDENTIAL.

WAR DIARY

OF

D.A.D.O.S., 21st Division.

FROM:- 1st November 1918.   TO:- 31st November 1918.

Army Form C. 2118.

WAR DIARY
or
INTELLIGENCE SUMMARY.
(Erase heading not required.)

Instructions regarding War Diaries and Intelligence Summaries are contained in F.S. Regs., Part II. and the Staff Manual respectively. Title pages will be prepared in manuscript.

December 1918. DAOOS 21st Division

Place	Date	Hour	Summary of Events and Information	Remarks and references to Appendices
BERLAIMONT	1/12/18		DAQMG called for report on delay in supply of boots and grindery. Truck containing boots & grindery arrived. DAQMG informed.	
do	2/12/18		Called on 1 Bn Lincoln Regt., 2 Bn Lincoln Regt.	
do	3/12/18		—	
do	4/12/18		Truck containing tools, clothing &c received but no boots or grindery arrived. Bar again hailing by wire.	
do	5/12/18			
do	6/12/18		Called on DAOOS V Corps and visited railhead. One truck boots cleared from railhead.	
do	7/12/18		One truck blanket cleared from railhead. Supplies of clothing to depots. to Field companies & Pioneers in new area.	
do	8/12/18		One truck grindery and clothing cleared from railhead. Stores still in shortage of boots.	
do	9/12/18		Instructions received from DAQMG to move to new area as WD not.	
do	10/12/18		Moved base to obtain vans and arranged to re-consign truck always advent to new railhead at AILLY-SUR-SOMME.	
do	13/12/18		Visited new area to find site for office and dumps.	
do	14/12/18		Moved office and dumps to MOLLIENS-VIDAME	

WAR DIARY
or
INTELLIGENCE SUMMARY.
(Erase heading not required.)

Army Form C. 2118.

Place	Date	Hour	Summary of Events and Information	Remarks and references to Appendices
MOLLIENS-VIDAME	15/12/18		Called at dump railhead at AILLY-SUR-SOMME	
	16/12/18		Truck X.28654 franc SARECHES received at AILLY-SUR-SOMME apparently in order but on examination contents were found to have been tampered with and a considerable quantity of its clothing stolen. Investigation showed that seals of seals had been changed. Matter reported to R.T.O.	
do	18/12/18		One truck general stores cleared from railhead. O.Q.F.18 pdr ammunition for A/95 Bde R.F.A. to replace no. 270 cartridges by 1000.	
do	19/12/18		Three trucks general stores cleared from railhead.	
do	20/12/18		One truck clothing and two trucks tannery stores from railhead.	
	21/12/18		Two lorry loads Ordnance delivered to Divisional Artillery.	
do			Cleared one truck general stores and one truck clothing from railhead. Returned two long tent poles to Madame Lens Robbes. Remainder O.Q.F. 18 pdr for C Bty 95 Bde to replace no.1096 cartridges of	
			I.O.M.	
do	22/12/18		S/conds duff reported for duty from 8th Division	

Army Form C. 2118.

WAR DIARY
or
INTELLIGENCE SUMMARY.
(Erase heading not required.)

Place	Date	Hour	Summary of Events and Information	Remarks and references to Appendices
MOLLIENS	23/12/18		Cleared 5 trucks (200x) blankets from railhead and dumped at A1244 S2/C. SOMME.	
VIGNACOURT	25/12/18		S. Cordo Bagg reported for duty from Advance Sup Coln No 74.	
	28/12/18		Demanded 30 Glass tops for Ross on instructions of ADME.	
	30/12/18		One truck gas clothing and 3 trucks general stores cleared from railhead.	
			Marchwood mr	

A6945 Wt. W14422/M1160 350,000 12/16 D. D. & L. Forms/C/2118/14.

9840.

CONFIDENTIAL.

WAR DIARY

OF

D.A.D. Ol S., 21st Division.

FROM:- 1st January 1919.   TO:- 31st January 1919.

Army Form C. 2118.

D.A.D.O.S.
21st DIVISION.

WAR DIARY
or
INTELLIGENCE SUMMARY.
(Erase heading not required.)

Instructions regarding War Diaries and Intelligence Summaries are contained in F. S. Regs. Part II. and the Staff Manual respectively. Title pages will be prepared in manuscript.

Place	Date	Hour	Summary of Events and Information	Remarks and references to Appendices
			January 1919.	
MOLLIENS-	Jan 1		Collected 220 Lamps Barrack Hanging from OO V Corps Troops.	
VIDANE	" 2		One trial general stores received from Base.	
	" 4		Collected 350 Lamps Ft. and 550 Cases Paillirens from OO V Corps Troops	
	" 5		Handed over to # Cavalry Brigade RHC	
			Snowchaddons	
	" 6		Proceeded on leave. E/20 Jerry	
	" 6		Visited No 4 Coy 21 Afrain. re accumulation of stones in Qm.t store	
			50 Stores Dapps received from Base + distributed to Units. 2 RFT Cloths	
			and one Storeman arrived to check from Havre. 1450 Cases	
			Paillares received from OO V Corps Troops	
	" 7		1 Truck Laundry Arrived from My Laundry. Visited Staff Capt 21 Div Arty.	
			Conference re the return of 2 Lewis Guns per Battery. Vide Third Army Letter	
			CJ500/3 dates 14-12-18. Classes 4 Tons Stores from Railhead 350	
			Large WS received from Base.	
	" 8		Delivered Cases Paillasses + 350 Lamps F.S to Units. Received by Programme	
			from FREVENT to belief for Div HQ to Road Cleaning. Visited 3 Ey 21"	
			Div. Trebin. re accumulation of stores at Qmrs stores.	

2nd Sheet

Army Form C. 2118.

WAR DIARY
or
INTELLIGENCE SUMMARY.
(Erase heading not required.)

D.A.D.O.S., ... DIVISION.

Place	Date 1919	Hour	Summary of Events and Information	Remarks and references to Appendices
MOLLIENS-VIDAME	Jan. 9	0600	One Army Lorry loaned to Camp Comdt. 21 Bn. to collect Wood from Armaments Pke.	
		4.10pm	Clothes arrived from Calais. One 15pr. received for 63rd Stable Bde.	
			Visited 12/13 MG and MQ R.E. store. No recommendation of store arrived in letter. Visited ADOS Office II Corps re Rif. pistols with Telescopic sight & 2 Lapelling lamps required urgently by 4th China Army.	
	10	1000	Cars Available. 10¢ Lewis Fd. 30¢ Lewis Pk. received for AA of	
			— 2 — Nors. Stores delivered to 21 Ani RA units.	
		1350	Visited 63rd Stable Bde. no recommendation of stores with QM. —	
			Advice received respecting from Sales GH2 DOS Report for IX 63rd Stable	
	11	5:00pm	Bofors gun 78ft received from Base Depot issued to R.E. & 300 to Div RE.	
		4:50	Frazier received from Base & distributes to units. Truck 1u-55-96 arrived from Base. No Windfall or Woodshed in Truck. Question taken up by RTO with OC Base. Carbide 9 Tons issue.	
	12		Cleaned tie Truck. Clean Clo: from Ruthless. Visited QM Stores of 1st Scouts Regt — built Fd. Amb. No accumulation of clothes exists. No impending move of Division — told gun	
	12.15		Visited Staff Capt. 21 Ani ARty re impending move of Division — told gun	

WAR DIARY or INTELLIGENCE SUMMARY

Army Form C. 2118.

D.A.D.O.S.

(Erase heading not required.)

Instructions regarding War Diaries and Intelligence Summaries are contained in F. S. Regs., Part II. and the Staff Manual respectively. Title pages will be prepared in manuscript.

Place	Date 1919	Hour	Summary of Events and Information	Remarks and references to Appendices
MOLLIENS - VIDAME	Jan 12		No information. Have applied for wire to corps with AOD II Corps re the transfer for Ordce services, in the event of the move taking place. AODIV Corps wired in particular re supply of spares. Position satisfactory except for Amb 6 & 7 which have not been received for a fortnight. Base stations have been by wire for these artys.	
	13	0830	Visits AOD II Corps re move of 23 DAC. Informed that as soon as the move is over the B3 actions should be known to OO XVII Corps keys.	
			2. O.O 7 18pm arrived at Railhead for 'A' B. 91-R21. 8o 11-24, 4794 dep. Capt. RA informed, who promises to arrange removal. Two trucks lathe chucks from Railhead (17tons) Visits AOMC Rept. Quistion re accumulation of store spares. Unit reports that all now known for concentration Corps have supply shed & that there were no complaints re tools or repairing material. Visits DDGMG Corps who was short of Grinding Requirements met from a small surplus in store. No accumulation of store spares.	
	14		1. 2 lorries called at all RFA units to collect "Returned Ordnance Stores"	

Army Form C. 2118.

WAR DIARY
or
INTELLIGENCE SUMMARY.
(Erase heading not required.)

D.A.D.O.S.
21st DIVISION.

Place	Date	Hour	Summary of Events and Information	Remarks and references to Appendices
MOLLIENS-VIDAME	15	0745	Delivered all available stores to RFA Units. Visited QM S' stores 21st Brigade Regt. No accumulation of stores evident. Received 80 Lewis gun with slings & distributed to Bdys. BSM's vice out ordered. One cover barrel 3" stokes Gun received for issue from OO II Bays. Canvas and issued to bty QMSgts. Replete for Guide.	
	16		Visited 9 Roy.S, 6.5 to Field Ambe., 14 MGs(pioneers) + 9th Leicesters Regt. Q.M. Stores. No accumulation of stores found. 9 Toms stokes cleaned from Ruilbène	
	17	0745	Sent 3 lorry loaded soiled underclothing to Railhead. Received in Truck Rifle shovels from Railhead delivered same to 110 Pioneers. Regt: bombers H.Q. M.G. Bn and see RFA units.	
	18	0745	Sent to lorry lamb Returned Ord 5 to Railhead. Ord: Room Genl Hawkes & Ord's HR Delivered stores to 21st Inf. Bn. 21st M.G. Coy + all RFA Units. 30th Field Survey B. R.R. and R.E. Habilitation leaves Third Army. Inspect from 3300 Ord 16.21 Ow for Administration for Ord. Stores. etc. Vide Ord: Third Army wire Z.F. 55" div. 17·11·19	

A6943 Wt. W14442/M1160 350,000 12/16⁶ D.D. & L. Forms/C/2118/14

WAR DIARY
INTELLIGENCE SUMMARY.
(Erase heading not required.)

Army Form C. 2118.

5th Div[?]

Place	Date 1919 Jan	Hour	Summary of Events and Information	Remarks and references to Appendices
MOLLIENS-VIDAME	19	1130	Visited ADOS I Corps Office and enquired re Demobilisation of R.A.O.C.	
		1545	One lorry loaded to H.Q. Div. Maj. Shuttleworth returned off leave and resumed duty as ACAOS 21 Div	
"	20		One truck general stores cleared from railway. mtReference Conds R&OC	
"	23		One truck clothing and general stores cleared from railway. R.V. Calibration from 3rd Army and 3rd Indian Lorry Batt.	
			Transferred from 33rd Div to 29th Div for supply of Ordnance Stores	
"	24		One lorry load stores despatches to Rue City	
"	25		One truck general stores cleared from railway	
"	28		" " " " " " "	
"	30		One truck containing lorry covering cleared from railway and away, delivered to Divl Artillery	

Shuttleworth Maj

CONFIDENTIAL.

WAR DIARY

OF

D. AND. O. S., 21st Division.

FROM:- 1st February 1919.   TO:- 28th February, 1919.

WAR DIARY or INTELLIGENCE SUMMARY

Army Form C. 2118.

No. 005 31 Division

February 1919.

(Erase heading not required.)

Instructions regarding War Diaries and Intelligence Summaries are contained in F. S. Regs., Part II. and the Staff Manual respectively. Title pages will be prepared in manuscript.

Place	Date	Hour	Summary of Events and Information	Remarks and references to Appendices
MOLLIENS-VIDAME	1/2/19		Called on Staff Captain 2nd Army Artillery, OC 94th Bde RFA and visited HQ C & D Batts 94th Bde RFA	
			One truck containing 200 Bucket Saline received & was not detailed to move from railhead	
do	2/2/19		One truck general stores drawn from railhead	
do	6/2/19		Called & talked to arrange for either to be changed or for trucks to be held up during thaw precaution	
			One truck general stores drawn then released	
do	9/2/19		Called on AQMG V Corps re question of Internment Billeting Hutting and accommodation here to view all at Longpré	
do	10/2/19		One truck general stores received from railhead	
do	11/2/19			
do	13/2/19		Marched about to Aux. Sup. Stores	
do	14/2/19		One truck general stores clothing Ord. drawn from railhead	
do	15/2/19		Called at Railhead Aux. Sup. Store and formed dump for about thing thaw precautions	

Army Form C. 2118.

WAR DIARY
or
INTELLIGENCE SUMMARY.
(Erase heading not required.)

Instructions regarding War Diaries and Intelligence Summaries are contained in F. S. Regs., Part II. and the Staff Manual respectively. Title pages will be prepared in manuscript.

Place	Date	Hour	Summary of Events and Information	Remarks and references to Appendices
MOLLIENS-VIDAME	16/2/19		One truck of general stores received and dumped at railhead.	
"	17/2/19			
"	18/2/19		All stores at railhead cleared by hired transport to dump at Molliens Vidame	
"	19/2/19		One truck of general stores received and forty places to Molliens	
"			Stores dumped at railhead	
"	20/2/19		Balance of stores cleared from railhead	
"	21/2/19		One truck general stores received at railhead	
"			General stores dumped at railhead and stores cleared by 21 Corps Column	
"			Instructions received to be in readiness to move to Longpre immediately	
"			Collecting stores at Longpre	
"	24/2/19		Called on A.D.O.S. V. Corps and discussed scheme for I.C.S.	
"			Called at railhead to arrange for return of 40 tons to Calais	
"	25/2/19		Cleared two truck general stores from railhead	
"	26/2/19		One kitchen travelling for 15 Bn Durham Light Infantry and one wagonette for 24th Divisional Signal Coy cleared from railhead	
"	27/2/19		Attended conference re I.C.S. at A.D.O.S. office and arranged to move to Longpre at an early date	

Army Form C. 2118.

WAR DIARY
or
INTELLIGENCE SUMMARY.
(Erase heading not required.)

Instructions regarding War Diaries and Intelligence Summaries are contained in F. S. Regs., Part II. and the Staff Manual respectively. Title pages will be prepared in manuscript.

Place	Date	Hour	Summary of Events and Information	Remarks and references to Appendices
NOLLIENS- VIDAME	7/4/19		Two tricks general orders cleared from residences. Ambushworth mops	

A6945 Wt W11422/M1160 350,000 12/16 D. D. & L. Forms/C./2118/14

WAR DIARY
or
INTELLIGENCE SUMMARY

(Erase heading not required.)

Army Form C. 2118.

March 1919

Place	Date	Hour	Summary of Events and Information	Remarks and references to Appendices
MOLLIENS-VIDAME	1/3/19		Two trucks with 3 18/pdr Barrage for B/95 Bde R.F.A., 3 18/pdr Barrage for B/95 Bde R.F.A. and 1 wagon load for 64 Field Ambulance arrived at railhead and unit-units to be called	
do	2/3/19		Called at railhead and 1.C.S. Longpré. An truck containing set. lids is for 21st M.G. Bn cleared from railhead and store delivered to unit	
do	3/3/19		Accompanied O.R.A.M.C. to Calais Park and 1.C.S. Longpré	
LONGPRE	4/3/19		Moved office and dump from MOLLIENS-VIDAME to LONGPRE. One truck general store cleared from railhead. Given instructions collecting Unions at Longpré for the receipt of supplies in accordance with para 12 Chapt X Army Suppliers Instructions	
do	5/3/19		Received visit from A.D.S. V Corps	
do	6/3/19		Received visit from A.D.S.T. Army and A.Q.M.S.V Corps. The hanger erected for the preservation of perishable stores was found to be very leaky and deeper inches for the proper expiring water effects to all concerned.	

WAR DIARY
or
INTELLIGENCE SUMMARY.
(Erase heading not required.)

Army Form C. 2118.

Place	Date	Hour	Summary of Events and Information	Remarks and references to Appendices
MOLLIENS-VIDAME	1/3/19		Two trucks with 2.18 pdr barrage for A/95 Bde RFA, 3.18 pdr barrages for B/95 Bde RFA and 1 wagon load of QF pdr for 64 Field Ambulance derailed at railhead and unfit wagonettes to collect	
	2/3/19		killed at railhead and ICS Longpré. An truck containing sub. items for 21st Mn Bty cleared from railhead and stores delivered to unit	
	3/3/19		Reconnoitred DRAMG & Cadre Park and ICS Longpré. Then office and dump from MOLLIENS-VIDAME to LONGPRE. The General states standard gauge railhead	
LONGPRE	4/3/19		Given permission to collect things at Longpré for the use of supplies advancing there in accordance with Para 7 C of X Army directive no 2918/A.A	
do	5/3/19		Received visit from A.O.O.S. V Corps	
do	6/3/19		Received visit from Major III Army and ADOS I Corps. The longer needed for the evacuation of prisoners does now found to be very heavy and further wires for the purpose required. Italian expected to all concerned	

Army Form C. 2118.

WAR DIARY
or
INTELLIGENCE SUMMARY.
(Erase heading not required.)

Place	Date	Hour	Summary of Events and Information	Remarks and references to Appendices
MOLLIENS- VIDAME	7/4/19		Two British general claims cleared from residence.	
			J M Beechworth Major	

WAR DIARY
or
INTELLIGENCE SUMMARY.
(Erase heading not required.)

Army Form C. 2118.

Instructions regarding War Diaries and Intelligence
Summaries are contained in F. S. Regs., Part II.
and the Staff Manual respectively. Title pages
will be prepared in manuscript.

Place	Date	Hour	Summary of Events and Information	Remarks and references to Appendices
LONGPRÉ	8/3/19		Received visit from A.D.O.S. V Corps.	
			Wire received from A.D.O.S. Corps placing embargo on returns to Calais for four days from yet not.	
			Lieut. Calais wired that railway would no longer accept truck labelled "See 80 for dispatch to 21 Div." Have wired to consign them to R.C.C. Hangest.	
			One truck containing 6 Coys general store issues from railhead.	
do	9/3/19		New roof for hangars arrived and erected. A.D.O.S. V Corps to hurry the erection of the cinema hut.	
do	10/3/19		Received visit from Corps Commander.	
do	12/3/19		One truck general stores clear from railhead. Called on A.D.O.S. V Corps. Visited Cadre Park to make a preliminary inspection of the equipment of the 1st Welsh Regt. in accordance with A.D.O.S. 0/584 of 3/3/19 but found that men were not fully acquainted with paras 45-53 Chap XIX of Army Boot Instns. Part I.	
do	13/3/19		All work arose to confirm that they are concerned with above paras. Called at Cadre Park and made a preliminary inspection of the equipment of the	

Army Form C. 2118.

WAR DIARY
or
INTELLIGENCE SUMMARY.
(Erase heading not required.)

Instructions regarding War Diaries and Intelligence Summaries are contained in F. S. Regs., Part II. and the Staff Manual respectively. Title pages will be prepared in manuscript.

Place	Date	Hour	Summary of Events and Information	Remarks and references to Appendices
Longpré	14/3/19		1Bn. Wiltshire Regt. Made a preliminary inspection of the equipment of the 2nd Bn Lincoln Regt and arranged for inspection by Inspection Staff to take place on Sunday morning at 10.30.	
"	15/3/19		Called on 1Bn Lincoln Regt. and 1Bn Wiltshire Regt. to arrange for equipment to be inspected on same date as the inspection of 2nd Bn Lincoln Regt.	
"	16/3/19.		Accompanied ADOS V Corps and inspected equipment of 1st and 2nd Bn of the Lincoln Regt.	
"	17/3/19.		Called on O.C. 1 East Yorks Regt. with regard to inspection of Regt Equipt. ADOS V Corps noted to arrange for inspection of 1 East Yorks Regt Equipment by Inspection Sn Corps Equipt at 10 A.M. on 21st inst.	
"	18/3/19		One fixed load of table arm forms despatched to O.C. L. of C. Troops. Made a preliminary inspection of the equipment of the 9th KORL, 1st East Yorkshire Regt and 6th 1st Brigade 3rd Divn.	
"	19/3/19		One truck load of table forms and tent d/sheet 5124-75 to Abbeville.	
"	20/3/19		One truck load of Bicycle debatable to O.O. Depot Haynville Dunkerque. Received article from ADOS 3rd Army.	

Army Form C. 2118.

WAR DIARY
or
INTELLIGENCE SUMMARY.

(Erase heading not required.)

Instructions regarding War Diaries and Intelligence Summaries are contained in F. S. Regs., Part II. and the Staff Manual respectively. Title pages will be prepared in manuscript.

Place	Date	Hour	Summary of Events and Information	Remarks and references to Appendices
Longpre	21/3/19		Despatched one truck bicycle to OD Depot Depot. Hornelle Brothers and one truck containing oil engine, wagon spares, wheels &c to the storehouse Calais.	
			Received visit from AOOSE Corps and inspected equipment of 21 Div Machine Gun Corps, 1 East Yorkshire Regt and 1 Wiltshire Regt.	
do	22/3/19		Despatch one truck bicycle to Hornelles 2 K.T. bodies received for 2 Lincoln Regt to replace 2 condemned by AOM	
do	23/3/19		One truck general store cleared from railhead. Despatched one truck of bicycles to OD Depot. Hornelle cont. 2 condemned K.T. bodies to 6th Wiltshire Yorkshire Calais.	
do	24/3/19		Made a preliminary inspection of equipment of 14 Div Train (S). Reserve count from Personal Commander. Despatching one truck bicycles to OD Depot Hornelles one box lined clothing, blankets, paillasse to Paris.	
do	26/3/19		One truck clothing &c cleared from railhead and one truck containing supplies for reaching tubular balance paillasse gum boots oxgen shoes &c despatched to Vendroux Calais.	
do	27/3/19		Received mail from Army Commander.	

Army Form C. 2118.

WAR DIARY
or
INTELLIGENCE SUMMARY.
(Erase heading not required.)

Place	Date	Hour	Summary of Events and Information	Remarks and references to Appendices
Songea	27/3/19		Received mail from ADMO and OS I Corps also ICS Ruturville. One K7 body of 1st Bombay Regt cleared from railroad and returned. One tired bicycle dispatches to DD Court depot Kigomille Bukoba and one truck conf. crockery to to DO Valelinia.	
do	29/3/19		One truck lamps, rope cloths + dispatches 6.00 Valelinia.	
do	30/3/19		One truck general stores cleared from railhead.	
do	31/3/19		Handed over to hind MX Corps RAOC and proceeded on leave. [signature] Superintendent Major	
do	"		Despatched six tons Tabbagarno to Boma. One truck supplies to Boma, Offices and dumps vacated by AOD I Corps. Beauregario. [signature] Lieut Col	

WAR DIARY
or
INTELLIGENCE SUMMARY.

Army Form C. 2118.

DADOS 21 Div and OO JCD Egypt. Ex. Corps - Sicily

Place	Date	Hour	Summary of Events and Information	Remarks and references to Appendices
Forgues	1/4/19	10.00	Visited Lieut Col. 21 DAC for preliminary inspection. Collected broken Marseille lorry — Col. 4th Gen R.F.A. Bn visited Ca 21 and Ca City.	
			Le Borne M the discards of lorries M.T. parts. Despatches on truck	
			Saddle Blanketh expeimenting to Paris	
"	2/4/19		Held preliminary inspection of C+D Batteries 95th Bde R.F.A. Visited Ca CCS on return re supply Reserve & lorries. AW 17th Bde	
			Unit moved to JCS Forgues for Ord. stores. 93.7.36 moved to ComDW.	
		12.00	Officer i/dump visited by AOd V Corps.	
		15.00	Officer i/dump inspected by DDOS Third Army.	
	3/4/19		Held preliminary inspection of M.T. 21 DAC, No +A,B,C+D Batt pullouts.	
			Arranged to Zotten drawfeelf, to be sent to Corps Park to transport	
			dewch. Blanketh & trackage. Despatches on truck Blanketh & Pure.	
"	4/4/19		Despatches on truck Blanketh, Gun Pullover, also one truck lorryung	
			to Bone. Storm Salvage (one) sent to Richard for Bone.	
"	6/4/19		Despatches one truck of more stores to Bone, mirror 21.24.50.21	
			unity by JCS for Ord. supplies. JCS visited by Brig. Gen N Command.	

A6945. Wt. W11492/M1160 350,000 12/6 D. D. & L. Forms/C.2118/14.

Army Form C. 2118.

WAR DIARY
or
INTELLIGENCE SUMMARY.
(Erase heading not required.)

Place	Date	Hour	Summary of Events and Information	Remarks and references to Appendices
Dieppe	5/4/19		RWOC 1 WO & 4 OR 1st Rft Bn arrived for duty. 2nd Lincoln Regt. 2nd Bn W Coy Rfts 2nd Bn W Coy Rfts returned from hosp & leave & admin dets	
			owing to entraining for U.K.	
	6/4/19		Visited the CCS & collected 20 Lee Enfield rifles, arms of DRR No. 3 Ammn. Received instruction for final inspection to be held on 8 - 4 - 19 for 118 OR 8 Lent 2 6 my Lee Enfd 15(KRR) 9th K Royal Rifles 62nd Brigade 14 NF (B). 6 B Gun 6 65 Field Ambce., 33rd Mobile Vet Sec.	
	7/4/19		Returns from trans and tels. rec. now from Lieut McCooper RAMC.	
	8/4/19		Railhead moved from Hangest to Longpré and one truck closed.	
	9/4/19		Inspected equipt of 62 & 110 Bde Hd Qrs, 6 & 7th Lincolnshire Regts, 15 trench mortars 9th KRR and 14 N.F. (Pioneers), 63, 64 & 65 Field Ambulances, 62nd Cavalry. Lieut Beaumont Edwards reported for duty from 2CBS. 2 trucks containing vehicles, trucks which, equipments, and stores destined to be sent Beaumont. 1 truck containing surplus stores, etc. looking to be to Motordam, and 1 truck supposed to go contain magazine	
	10/4/19		3 Truck vehicle despatched to Beaumarais, 2 to Paris and 1 not Mag Station	

A6945 Wt. W14421/M1160 350,000 12/16 D. D. & L. Forms/C.2118/14

WAR DIARY
or
INTELLIGENCE SUMMARY.
(Erase heading not required.)

Army Form C. 2118.

Instructions regarding War Diaries and Intelligence Summaries are contained in F. S. Regs., Part II. and the Staff Manual respectively. Title pages will be prepared in manuscript.

Place	Date	Hour	Summary of Events and Information	Remarks and references to Appendices
Longpre	1/4/19		4 truck vehicles dispatched to Etaples Germanies 1 truck surplus stores to Abbeville	
			1 truck to No 8 Reg. Stg.	
do	2/4/19		5 truck vehicles dispatched to Dieppe, Beauview. 1 truck Table forms etc to Rue Wagner, 1 truck clothing etc to Paris and one truck surplus stores to Folklore	
			One truck general store stores from canteen	
do	3/4/19		One truck jumble store and 1 truck with RE boxy chains farm implements	
do	4/4/19		2 truck vehicles 1 truck surplus store to Abbeville and 1 truck to No 8 Stg. Workshops	
			Inspection equipment of 12/13 Bn Northumberland Regt, 1st Cheshire and 64 TMB, 126 Field Coy and by Lieut. Col 14 Y. 14/8 and 183 Coys RE & S	
do	15/4/19		Despatched one truck Table braths etc. to No 11 Ord. Depot and one truck to No 8 Ord. Depot	
			Inspected equipt of 78 Field Coy 57 & 53 Field Amb 29 Mobile Vet Sec 17 Dv. Signal Co, HQ R.A. B.C & D Bys 95 Brigade RFA and 50-bi Trench Mortar Bty.	

Army Form C. 2118.

WAR DIARY
or
INTELLIGENCE SUMMARY.
(Erase heading not required.)

Place	Date	Hour	Summary of Events and Information	Remarks and references to Appendices
Rouxpres	16/4/19		One truck despatched to No 8 Ord Depot	
	17/4/19		Inspected equipment of 51 Bde HB. Received visit from OROS 3rd Army and Brig Gen Stokes Baker CRLO. Handed over to Lieut Beaumont Edmonds and proceeded to take up duty as DOOS Amiens Sub Area.	Smoochwood Major
	18/4/19		Inspected equipment of 51 TMB, 78th - 79th Bgds RFA - HQ 17 Div RA	
	19/4/19		2 Truck loads to Calais Salvage PR. Inspected 110 TMB (x) attd. X 61 Div. Two. 1 Truck load to Calais. Went from Sup Dump. Inspected equipment 21 DAC and X,Y,21 TMB. 1 Truck load to No 8 Ord Depot. 3 Flat beds received from TM Gun PR with limbers	
	20/4/19		Reserves for obsolete chains.	
	21/4/19		Inspected 62 TMB light. 1 Flat truck from labour 2 to from Sp thompson Ordnance Workshop Bottle 51 b Beauvois	(No 2a/5)
	22/4/19			
	23/4/19		Inspected Equipment of 9 HB,RFA HQ 12 Div 45th Bde, HQ 13th TMB. Red.load truck from Sales Depot. 1 to ship G OD.	XY TMB 17 Bde xx Flat Lorie

Army Form C. 2118.

WAR DIARY
or
INTELLIGENCE SUMMARY.
(Erase heading not required.)

Instructions regarding War Diaries and Intelligence Summaries are contained in F. S. Regs., Part II. and the Staff Manual respectively. Title pages will be prepared in manuscript.

Place	Date	Hour	Summary of Events and Information	Remarks and references to Appendices
Longfre	24/4/19		1 Closed truck despatched to Beaumarais	
"	25/4/19		Inspected equipment of 52 Fld Amb, 153 AFA, HQ 1, 2, 3 & 4 Battys, a squad sec. Armrd Cd HQ 21 Div, HQ 21 Div Engineers, HQ 21 Div art. Visit from ADOS & ADOS 3rd Area	
			despatched one closed truck to Calais Palluture	
	26/4/19		Visit from ADOS. Arrived SAA Res. 5/1st trucks with wagons from 9th & Beaufroy	
			despatches one closed to 11 OD	
			Recd one closed truck from Calais despatched one closed to Palluture	
	27/4/19		Inspected equipment of 21 Sqndl 6 RE, 77 Field GRE, HQ 17 Bde RE, HQ 2 Bty	
	28/4/19		17 Div Train. Despatched one closed truck to Calais Palluture & one to Calais Port (4:45pm)	
	29/4/19		1 Closed Truck to No 8 Ord Depot.	
	30/4/19		Recd 1 flat truck & 1 closed from Calais. Desp. closed and flat to Calais. Visit from ADOS	
	1/5/19		Inspected Equipment of HQ 17 Bde	
	2/5/19		1 Closed truck for Calais Palluture	
	3/5/19		1 flat truck with 8 lorries from GPH Calais Calais & closter head from 110TS	
	4/5/19		Sent over 18 pdr lorries to H.M. Carders. 1 flat truck from Calais	
	5/5/19		1 Closed truck from Calais. 1 closed to No 8 OD	

(A78531) Wt. W8091/M1672 350,000 4/17 D. D. & L., London, E.C. Sch. 82a Forms/C2118/14

WAR DIARY
or
INTELLIGENCE SUMMARY.
(Erase heading not required.)

Army Form C. 2118.

Instructions regarding War Diaries and Intelligence Summaries are contained in F. S. Regs., Part II. and the Staff Manual respectively. Title pages will be prepared in manuscript.

Place	Date	Hour	Summary of Events and Information	Remarks and references to Appendices
Longpré	6/5/19	—	1 Closed truck from Calais 1 do for Calais Pot.	
"	7/5/19		1 do to to Dieppe with Blankets with mens General Crosby 16th Ep. Rft.	
	8/5/19		Nil	
	9/5/19		Nil	
	10/5/19		1 Closed Truck R.J.C. Delivery Ford Return 1 do to E. O.D. Visit from D.D.O.T. Let. Cnn.	
	11/5/19		Visit from Col Tufnell and Col Heape	
	12/5/19		Visit from Col Heape also Col Liveston	
	13/5/19		Rec'd 4 flat trucks from Calais Orfolds 1 closed to Dieppe	
	14/5/19		Rec'd 2 closed trucks from Calais 24 F heavies reported for duty from Calais	
	15/5/19		Nil	
	16/5/19		Nil	
	17/5/19		2 Closed Trucks for Calais 1 closed to Etaples N.K.R.D.	
	18/5/19		Nil	
	19/5/19		1 Flat Truck from Calais 1 Closed Abancourt	
	20/5/19		3 Flat Trucks from Calais with Wagons & Limbers Rec'd from Calais 1 closed to O.D. Dieppe Government	
	21/5/19		1 Closed to do 8 O.D Visit from Col Heape - D. Staff	

Army Form C. 2118.

WAR DIARY
or
INTELLIGENCE SUMMARY.
(Erase heading not required.)

Instructions regarding War Diaries and Intelligence Summaries are contained in F. S. Regs., Part II. and the Staff Manual respectively. Title pages will be prepared in manuscript.

Place	Date	Hour	Summary of Events and Information	Remarks and references to Appendices
Longpré	24/4/19		1 Closd truck despatches to Beauvais	
"	25/4/19		Inspected equipment of 52 Fld Amb. 153 AFA HQ 7,2,3 + 4 Batty. a Signal sec. arrived	
			HQ 21 Div. HQ 21 Div Engineers. HQ 21 Div Art. Visit from DDOS ADOS 3rd area	
			despatches one clsd truck to Calais Falstlhirsn.	
	26/4/19		Visit from DADOS Amiens S.A. Recd 5/4at trucks with wagons from GPH u. Busigny	
			despatches one clsd to 11 GD	
	27/4/19		Recd one clsd truck from Calais despatches one clsd to Valentines	
	28/4/19		Inspected equipment of 21 Sqnd L6 RE, 77 Fld C.RE, HQ 17 Div RE, HQ 21 Div Engr.	
			17 Div Train despatches one clsd truck to Calais Valentines + one to Calais Pnt (1½DX Fuses)	
	29/4/19		1 closd truck to Tos 8 Ord Depot	
	30/4/19		Recd 1/flat truck + 1 clsd from Calais. Despatches one flat to Calais visit from DDS.	
	1/5/19		Inspection equipment of HQ 17 Div	
	2/5/19		1 closd truck for Calais Falstlhirsn	
	3/5/19		1 flat truck with 8 lorries from GPH + C Soss from Calais + 18 pdrs 1 closd to Busigny Road from 11 GDS	
	4/5/19		Sent over 18 pdr lorries to H.M Canders. 1 flat truck from Calais	
	5/5/19		1 closd truck from Calais. 1 closd to Tos 8 OD	

(A78531) Wt. W809/M1072 350,000 4/17 Sch. 52a Forms/C2118/14
D. D. & L., London, E.C.

Army Form C. 2118.

WAR DIARY
or
INTELLIGENCE SUMMARY.
(Erase heading not required.)

Instructions regarding War Diaries and Intelligence Summaries are contained in F. S. Regs., Part II. and the Staff Manual respectively. Title pages will be prepared in manuscript.

Place	Date	Hour	Summary of Events and Information	Remarks and references to Appendices
Longpre	6/5/19	—	1 closed truck from Calais 1 do for Calais Pol.	
"	7/5/19	—	1 " " " " "	
	8/5/19	—	Nil	
	9/5/19	—	Nil	
	10/5/19	—	1 Closed Truck & 2 P.O. railway Trucks from 16 to 8 OD. Verify from SDD to station	
	11/5/19	—	Boat from Col Tilquete and Col Herr	
	12/5/19	—	Nil from Col heads, also Col Lincoln	
	13/5/19	—	Recd 4 flat trucks from Calais Dispatches 1 closed to Dieppe	
	14/5/19	—	Recd 2 closed trucks from Calais. W.O. P. heures reported for duty from Aldershot	
	15/5/19	—	Nil	
	16/5/19	—	Nil	
	17/5/19	—	2 Closed Trucks for Calais 1 Closed to Tilque & L.O. N. 8 O.D.	
	18/5/19	—	Nil	
	19/5/19	—	1 Mtr. Truck from Calais 1 Closed Elsenhorne	
	20/5/19	—	3 flat trucks from Calais will train one closed 1 cond from Calais 1 do to OO Supp Command	
	21/5/19	—	1 Closed to no 8 OD Visit from Col Messer ~ 8 Staff	

Army Form C. 2118/4.

WAR DIARY
or
INTELLIGENCE SUMMARY

Army Form C. 2118.

(Erase heading not required.)

Place	Date	Hour	Summary of Events and Information	Remarks and references to Appendices
Longpré	22/5/19	—	Visit from the Agents. 1 ClO2 truck to No 8 OD	
"	23/5/19	—	Wanted 155 Brigade 2 Cow trucks to OD Bergues	
	24/5/19		Stat for known trek for O/C Stay to Armentières	
	25/5/19		Nil	
	26/5/19		India Post Corps re-establd field bttn for tribute for 1 shortage fr Calais	
	27/5/19		Unit for 20 BTS Armoured Column	
	28/5/19		1 ClO2 truck for Calais. 1 ClO2 truck to 8 OD	
	29/5/19		1 ClO2 truck to No OD but Kallie Ill (MO2) unexpd out	
	30/5/19		Visited Pol Remy 10 2nd Stay s Dick to Mont	
	31/5/19		Was picked up at Pol Remy. Lorries 5/1 to OD fr loadings	

30/5/19

www.ingramcontent.com/pod-product-compliance
Lightning Source LLC
Chambersburg PA
CBHW081354160426
43192CB00013B/2408